Contents

New Thinking in School Geography

Her Majesty's Stationery Office 1972

98331

SBN 11 270098 5

Introduction

Geography teachers find themselves in an unstable period of rapid change. The disciples of change belong to two quite different persuasions. First there are those who are concerned that 'the thread linking research, university teaching and school teaching, a thread already pulled taut, should not be allowed to part.'[1] These are the academic geographers whose devotion is, naturally, to the subject. Secondly there are the educationists dedicated to curriculum reform who ask 'What is important to society and the individual?', and who warn of the 'risk that a young school leaver may contract out of a school situation which is no longer of any consequence to him' because 'his lack of academic abilities has ruled him out of a school curriculum dominated by external examinations.'[2]

The geography teacher is both geographer and educationist and his loyalties are primarily to all the pupils he teaches, ranging from the intellectually brilliant to those whose natural and environmental endowments are meagre. He must do justice to the one-twentieth of the school population who now offer the subject at Advanced level and the one-quarter who attempt the Ordinary level examinations for the General Certificate of Education, and the growing numbers who work for the Certificate of Secondary Education. He must also provide satisfying courses for the large number who do not aim at examination success in the subject.

What the geography teacher needs, most of all, to assist him is fundamental research into the capacities of boys and girls to deal with the knowledge, skills, concepts and abstract ideas with which he is concerned and the means and progressive stages by which they may be successfully mastered. It may be some years before the results of research of this kind are available. In the meantime teachers must depend on the wisdom and experience that is widely spread among their ranks, and this pamphlet is an attempt to collate current thinking as an interim support in a period when the advocates of change are unusually clamant and compelling.

[1] P. Haggett *Frontiers in Geographical Teaching*: Ed. Chorley and Haggett. Methuen 1965.

[2] 'Working Paper No. 11: *Society and the Young School Leaver*' Schools Council HMSO 1967.

Throughout the evolution of geographical teaching in schools three continuing problems have called for solution—selection, methods and structure:

(a) Selection is concerned with content. There is so much geography to teach that a process of choosing is inevitable. If too much is attempted the coverage is superficial; if the wrong things are chosen interest fades. Relevance and economy of selection are essential.

(b) Methods of teaching are closely linked with content and the capacities of pupils to learn. As books, teaching aids and access to the outside world have been improved the variety of methods available has increased. The richer the means at his disposal the more wary must the teacher be that means do not take the place of ends, and the greater must be his perception of the ends that his resources are designed to serve.

(c) Structure is concerned with the relationships and systems that geographical studies depend on to bring an embarrassingly varied mass of data within the comprehension of the pupils. Too often it has been said that geography is a series of descriptive accounts without internal logic or discipline. Yet economy of thought requires pattern and order. The teacher's problem is to identify the kinds and degrees of discipline which are appropriate to his pupils at each stage.

'A period of rapid evolution in a discipline occurs', writes P. J. Ambrose[3], 'when a sizeable minority of people within it become dissatisfied either with its intellectual content, or with the value of its contribution to society, or both'. The many new kinds of courses which are to be found in schools testify to the dissatisfaction of geography teachers. A continent-by-continent survey of the world, the division of countries into stereotyped self-contained regions, and simplified versions of advanced text-books on physical geography are no longer universally accepted as suitable fare. The pupil who has been drilled to give five reasons for the cotton industry in Lancashire or trained to compare and contrast the Mississippi and St. Lawrence Basins may well ask what these exercises have to do with understanding the modern world. If geography is to make a contribution to society it must attend to real problems rather than academic exercises. If the excessive load of memorisation is to be reduced it should be concerned with principles as well as facts. And if the geography learned in schools is to be of value in adult life it should awaken an interest in the world of today and provide tools of learning which can be used to understand the world of tomorrow.

---

[3] *Concepts in Geography*: *Analytical Human Geography*. Longmans 1969.

In the current reassessment of the role of the geography teacher changes are proposed which will necessitate the use of new criteria in the selection and methodology of courses.

1

Why Change?

'Geography today has not lost its old interests but it has greatly deepened them. Geography is still interested in the earth's surface as the home of man, still concerned with the where of life: but nowaday a simple memory of locational facts, a gazetteer, will no longer do. The student must have a deeper understanding of why objects are located where they are. The earth is not randomly arranged. Locations of cities, rivers, mountains, political units are not scattered helter-skelter in whimsical disarray. There exists a great deal of spatial order, of sense, on our maps and globes.' (William Bunge: *Theoretical Geography;* second edition 1966; University of Lund.)

Teachers of geography are well aware that they are caught up in a whirlwind of change; but no more than teachers of mathematics, science, English, modern languages, and other subjects. Indeed many of them are active in generating change through the medium of associations such as the Geographical Association, CSE subject committees, the Schools Council, local gatherings of many sorts and sizes, and conferences and short courses run by various organisations. There is no national consolidated list of the agencies involved or of their activities, but in any recent year hundreds of groups of geographers will have gathered together for single meetings or series of meetings concerned with promoting the quality of their contribution to education and the incorporation of new knowledge and ideas in school curricula. Some have co-operated with the BBC or ITV in broadcast lessons, and others with publishers in producing new kinds of text-books and work-books. To some the vistas revealed by new styles of geography are an exhilarating proof of the adaptability of the subject to the needs of a new and increasingly complex world; to others changes, which are thought to be too rapid and ill-considered, arouse feelings of trepidation or personal inadequacy. Yet geographers, whether radical or conservative in outlook, have never rested for long on an established position, as a glance at articles and books published over the last thirty or forty years on the teaching of geography will show. Older members of the teaching profession will recall the efforts made by Fairgrieve, Stambridge and others to bring 'realism' to the ordered body of systematic and regional geography which was gaining general acceptance in schools during the first three decades of the century; they will remember with gratitude the improving supplies of visual and audio-visual materials which have become available, and the more recent sample-studies, the farm studies of the Association of Agriculture, the Ship-Adoption scheme and other aids which have made realism more easy to achieve; they will look back on the advocacy by Wooldridge, Hutchinson and others of field teaching and field work as a proper basis of learning, and on the stimulus that two successive Land Utilisation Surveys have offered to examine the real world; they will ponder again on the arguments for 'concentric schemes' and for the 'integrated' or 'incidental' teaching of physical geography within regional frameworks. And as though this were not enough they are now confronted with suggestions for more fundamental and far-reaching modifications of their educational practice. Some may pursue their thinking in isolation, others in groups in the department of a large school, in the new Teachers' Centres, or in committees and conferences. Those who find the going difficult may take consolation from the quotation with which this chapter begins, for the 'new geography' is, in many senses, still firmly rooted in the old; we still explore the same territory but some of the instruments we use are unfamiliar, some of our objectives are different.

The Changing World

No matter how immutable the physical world may appear to be when viewed over a short period of time (apart from such catastrophes as earthquakes, volcanic eruptions, landslides and storms) there is evidence of significant modification in climate[1] in historical times which will help boys and girls to appreciate the importance for human activity of comparatively small fluctuations in temperature or rainfall regimes. Yet these changes fade to nothingness when thought is given to the rapidity with which human endeavour is altering the face of the earth or the style of life of communities. This is a theme that has attracted many writers during this century, of whom Ritchie Calder[2] and Carlo Cipolla[3] may serve as two recent examples. Not only do political frontiers change (or lie in a state of uncertain suspension) but the name of states themselves change as well as towns and other features. Madagascar becomes the Malagasy Republic, Northern Rhodesia Zambia, Tibet Hsi Tsang, Leopoldville Kinshasa, Hamilton River Churchill River. Where previously there

---

[1] See H. H. Lamb, *The English Climate*. English Universities Press 1964.
[2] R. Calder, *The Inheritors*. Heinemann 1961.
[3] Carlo Cipolla, *The Economic History of World Population*. Penguin 1962.

were few or no inhabitants new towns arise such as Raurkela, Kuwait, Angarsk or Cumbernauld. Aluminium ore brings a new importance to Weipa in Queensland, iron ore to Schefferville in Quebec, oil to Hassi Messaoud in Algeria or Zelten in Libya; and the number of new water-control projects with hydro-electric power stations or irrigation works is legion. For details of these and similar instances of man's manipulation of his environment the geographer is glad to turn to such handy reference sources as the annual 'Geographical Digest' (Philip) or the appropriate pages of 'Geography', the journal of the Geographical Association. The facts of a developing world may be simple, but from them flow consequences for population redistribution, trade, and changes in the balance of economic activity that the geography teacher must interpret. There are, however, other movements afoot which must impinge upon his thinking and which call for a professional reappraisal of his task.

The Universities and the School

Teachers of geography will be aware of the way in which University thinking has enlarged its scope. Side by side with advanced textbooks, standard works and reference books dealing with the familiar themes of physical, historical, social and economic geography and an increasing number of regional studies, have appeared a large number of works by geographers, dealing with urban and political geography, the geography of settlement, specialised aspects of economic geography, and applied geography which appear in some senses to break with or to grow beyond, past traditions. Works such as 'Frontiers in Geographical Teaching' (Ed. Chorley and Haggett: Methuen), 'Locational Analysis in Human Geography' (Haggett: Arnold) and 'Quantitative Geography' (Cole and King: Wiley) draw together some of the threads of developing thought among geographers and show how they have been enriched by more refined techniques of collecting and handling data as well as by the search for new relationships in the distribution of elements on the surface of the earth.

In the short compass of an article in the Times Educational Supplement of 26th May 1967, Professor K. C. Edwards summarised the main features of the post-war expansion of geographical work. 'While important advances had been made in geomorphology and biogeography it was in human geography and in various aspects of applied geography that progress had been greatest; and in the social and economic fields there had been an almost revolutionary advance. Applied geography, he claimed, had increasingly turned its attention to the problems confronting modern society in urban and highly industrialised communities at one extreme and those facing the inhabitants of underdeveloped countries at the other'. Its role lay 'in the context of specific problems like those encountered in physical planning, resource development and conservation'. He pointed out the need for a better knowledge of some aspects of mathematics enabling quantification to be applied to data in both physical and socio-economic studies.

What are the effects of these widening horizons upon the work of the schools? In the first place there is a new generation of graduate teachers of geography and teachers trained in Colleges of Education who bring with them outlooks and skills which may be strange to their older colleagues. Some of these skills may be of great value in the schools, some may prove to have little application to the education of many boys and girls. Certainly new methods and fields of study are worth exploring at school level for geography has been invigorated repeatedly in the past from the interest that can be aroused in pupils by fresh transfusions of thought. It, would, however, be as unwise to attempt to reform school geography on the lines of an expanding University discipline as it would be to reject out of hand elements which, can, with thought, be profitably tailored to school use. It is for teachers to discover, by experiment, the ways in which school geography can benefit from innovation in the Universities.

In the second place there is the question of knowledge which has come from the renewed investigation of well established concepts. Nowhere is this more important than in the field of physical geography. Recent work on rivers, ice, shorelines, air-masses and other topics, in which preconceived ideas have held sway for many years, has revealed the falsity of some of the doctrine which has been recorded in text-books and taught in schools.[4] Fortunately communication between the Universities and schools has never been better, and the willingness of University dons to meet teachers and discuss with them the implications of research, insofar as they amend commonly held opinions, has hastened the process by which knowledge can be brought up-to-date. Their willingness, too, to demonstrate techniques of work has enabled many teachers to face the prospect of change with some confidence.

Changing Ideas on Education Practice
Many of the changes in teachers' ideas of how children learn stem from the work of Piaget and Innhelder which has gained wide

---

[4] See articles by G. H. Dury and J. C. Pugh in *Geography*, January 1963 and January 1964, respectively.

currency in recent years. As far as geography is concerned it offers guide lines for thinking about what should be taught, and how and when, in general, though not in specific, terms.

For a possible application of these ideas to the teaching of certain aspects of geography, particularly in the primary schools, the reader is referred to an article by A. H. McNaughton in the Educational Review of November 1966[5] from which the following quotations may be relevant. 'The quality of thinking of children of a particular stage differs significantly from that of children at other stages. Human characteristics of active exploration of the environment and of being ready for change are the main factors which allow for movement from one stage to the next. No teacher can be sure that the material that has been read or the pictures shown will have the same effects on all children. Each child will bring to such experiences perceptions which are conditioned by his own past and made inflexible by his own stage of mental development. Whatever the effect of these perceptions may be they will tend to be accepted unquestioningly by the young unless, of course, the teacher is aware of this situation and takes steps to find out as early as possible just what is going on in the minds of his pupils. Most primary school children will not, without considerable prompting, stand back from what they read about people and compare them with others and with themselves'.

Geography courses in primary schools which were widely followed for several decades are thus called into question. An orderly series of vignettes of family life in other lands, selected with a view to demonstrating typical human responses to the major climatic regions of the world, illustrated with photographs and brightly coloured pictures to vivify oral teaching or textbook accounts, possessed for the teacher an orderly sequence and admitted of bold comparisons, but they seldom had any of the desired impact unless a great deal of time and trouble were taken to analyse the children's reactions in detailed and unhurried discussion. Too often the repetition by children of approved answers to questions from the teacher has passed for evidence of understanding. Direct experience by the children of their own environment, enquiry into questions raised by themselves as well as those suggested by the teacher, opportunities to talk about what they have seen and heard, and personal records of their impressions rather than class exercises provide a surer foundation for advance than set lessons with predetermined beginning, middle and end.

At the secondary stage abstract ideas and broad generalisations are shown to be unprofitable in the early stages unless they can be the

---

[5] *Piaget's Theory and Primary School Social Studies.*

B

results of deductions made by the pupils rather than the teachers, from actual examples. Many geography teachers have discovered that some general principles, particularly in physical geography, taught in the first or second years of the secondary school have been invested with misconceptions, or are falsely applied to inappropriate situations, and frequently have to be taught again in the fourth or fifth years when the pupils' minds are more mature. This is not to argue for the abandonment of abstract ideas and generalisations, for these represent economies of thought which are necessary if geography is not to be a mass of memorised fact. Rather it argues for teaching in which the pupil is actively engaged in arriving at general concepts which are appropriate to his level of understanding.

J. S. Bruner,[6] basing his thinking upon the work of Piaget, claims that 'knowledge one has acquired without sufficient structure to tie it together is knowledge that is likely to be forgotten'.

His views have strongly influenced authors engaged in the American High School project, who have produced a number of assignments of work in geography, in which concrete operations and hypotheses are included.

New Patterns of Educational Organisation and Examinations

We have for some twenty years been accustomed in the public sector of schools to a break in education at the age of eleven with two distinct layers of primary and secondary education, the secondary layer being split into two main columns, one for the Grammar schools and one for the Modern. True there were a small number of Technical schools and a few but increasing number of Comprehensives. In the early 1950s most geography teachers in Secondary schools thought in terms of Grammar school courses or non-grammar school courses, and the popular belief was that the academic work was embraced in the former and the non-academic in the latter. Such a simple black-and-white differentiation could not persist for long. There followed a period of adjustment in which Modern schools strengthened the quality of disciplined thinking, particularly for their abler pupils, and prepared many of them for the General Certificate of Education. As Comprehensive schools increase in number and Middle schools become established many geography teachers will need to make a fresh appraisal of their tasks.

The recent advent of the Certificate of Secondary Education afforded teachers the opportunities and responsibilities of devising new kinds

---

[6] J. S. Bruner, *The Process of Education.* Harvard University Press, 1965.

of examinations suited to a large proportion of their pupils. A comparison of geography Mode 1 syllabuses for 1966 and 1970 reveals the extent to which teachers have benefited from early experience and modified the examinations to suit their pupils; field work, individual topics of study, the use of atlases, facility in handling statistics or 'reading' pictures, greater selectivity in regional studies and a reduction in the load of memorisation all indicate a movement away from text-book learning towards a process in which the pupil is doing more and thinking more himself. In addition the adoption of Mode III examinations permits an intensive study of the local region as part of the examination; and where a group of schools in a locality offer a 'group Mode III' syllabus the work of preparing the examination, which inevitably makes heavy demands, can be shared among a body of teachers.

2

The Purposes and Scope of School Geography

Geography and Education (HMSO 1960) deals with the growth of geography as a discipline and a school subject. Its pages can still be read with profit by all who teach the subject. Geography, well taught, has much to offer boys and girls in developing powers of observation, analysis and interpretation of various kinds of data including maps. Teachers of geography share with teachers of history, science, English and other subjects certain common interests in educational processes relating to the total environment, natural and man-made; but they also have their special contribution which is distinctive. Put in its simplest terms they are concerned with helping their pupils to know:

(a) where places are
(b) what they are like
(c) what life is like in them
(d) how and why they are changing
and (e) the ways in which places are linked with one another

Without further qualification this could argue for a programme which might provide a large store of knowledge but little understanding of a dynamic world.

As boys and girls look around them they see a neighbourhood which is subject to constant modification; its future depends on decisions which are being taken, some at local and others at national or international level. All over the world neighbourhoods and peoples are subject to forces of innovation. Great issues in Britain such as those affecting the special regions, the use of water resources, motorways, conservation, .the export trade and relations with Europe and the Commonwealth have their counterparts in other countries. If geography can reduce an apparent chaos of unstable spatial distributions into some recognisable order it will have played a significant part in helping pupils to understand their world. This will involve not only a study of social, economic and political forces but also the varying ways in which they come to terms with natural conditions such as land-forms, climate, natural vegetation and soils. Thus while

8

the study of place is a central theme the justification of school geography lies in the context in which places are studied.

The purist may ask for a definition of 'places', does the word cover countries, or villages, or regions of one sort or another? And what is meant by 'knowing where'? In what terms can position be defined? Again what factors should be taken into account in describing 'what places are like'? What emphasis should be placed on the visual aspects of landscape, countryside and towns, what on the cycle of the seasons or the odours and sounds that may be as characteristic of some places as their appearance? And what do we mean by 'life'? Does the term comprehend domestic and economic activity alone, or should the social customs, recreations, religions, arts, music and political institutions also find a place? Some may ask whether the analysis of spatial distributions and of the complex relationships and processes that geographers study are to be omitted.

Answers to questions such as these depend on the fact that school geography covers a vast range of experiences. At the one end of the scale are young children looking wide-eyed for the first time at the ploughshare turning the earth; hearing for the first time words like furrow, plough, arable and crop, and asking why and how often the farmer does this and how long it will take the crop to grow. At the other end are sixth-formers on the verge of adulthood, conducting a survey of geomorphological features or urban functional zones on the ground, or consulting a variety of source materials with a view to analysing economic or population changes in a remote country or region, and possibly discussing the factors which will help them to arrive at a valid delimitation of a 'region'. In the continuum of learning that stretches from the young child to the school leaver the teacher looks for commonsense methods of dealing with the where, what and how of geography, and these, if they are to be effective, must relate to the children's degree of understanding, their existing stock of knowledge and the resources available both in and around the school.

The situation is rendered more complex for the teacher because he alone does not control the children's sources of information. There is no simple base from which he can move forward without outside interference, planning each new vista as a rationally ordered step from the last. Not only do homes, parents and experience of travel vary; exposure to the means of mass communication affords for all an indiscriminate array of glimpses of distant parts and of ideas about the world. The child may know the facts that the world is round and that it travels round the sun long before his senses can support or interpret them; he becomes aware that places like Japan,

Australia and Hawaii exist possibly before he has any understanding
of his father's place of work and the intervening few miles of town or
countryside. As the Plowden Report[1] says, 'the cinema, the press and
most of all television have made available to everyone a general
visual knowledge of the world such as was impossible for adults, let
alone children, before their invention'. Thus at any stage the teacher
may find that individual pupils have something to contribute to the
work in hand; sometimes their knowledge is firmly comprehended,
sometimes confused and in need of clarification, and sometimes
quite new to the teacher himself.

There are, however, spheres in which it is possible for the teacher to
aim at a commonly shared body of direct experience, and this arises
from studies of the home environment, which can be carried out with
varying degrees of sophistication. For younger children the home
area may be the only one which they can comprehend with the whole
of their senses, and for many the separate facets of the local district
and their interlocking relationships provide the only yardsticks by
which they can measure and interpret the world beyond. 'Their whole
environment is the book from which, without conscious effort, they
are constantly enriching their memory against the time when their
judgment will be able to profit by it.'[2] For younger children 'Their
whole environment' has a special significance and it is to the primary
school that we now turn.

[1] *Children and their Primary Schools.* HMSO 1967 (See Chapter 17).
[2] *Emile.* Rousseau.

3

Younger Children

'Home is where we start from. As we grow older the world becomes stranger, the pattern more complicated'. T. S. Elliot (East Coker).

To children up to the age of eight or nine the concept of place even in an area as large as a parish, a sizeable village, or the district of a town served by a primary school may be hard to grasp as a whole. Yet there is an infinity of interest in its parts. Constant visits to a shop or park, to relatives, to church and to school may result in familiarity with short journeys and isolated elements in the local scene even with a child as young as four or five. But the spatial relationships between them do not emerge until several years later. Nor, with young children, is it easy to dissociate 'geographical' from 'non-geographical' features. Their bounding curiosity moves from one thing to another, from people to their clothing, the way they speak, their bicycles or cars, or their pet dogs; from the road sweeping-vehicle to a passing lorry or bus; from the shop windows to a waiting baby in a perambulator. This is the time when the memory is being enriched and vocabulary learned and tested so that communication of what is remembered may be achieved.

Vocabulary and Records

The enlargement and refinement of vocabulary is one of the most important aims for the teacher. Trees may be differentiated into oaks, holly, hawthorn, ash and elm; vehicles are distinguished as lorries, tankers, vans and cars; a stream yields the terms current, flow, bank, bed and sediment; and older children may begin to recognise several of the major cloud types, the breeds of cattle or the crops on a farm, and the various kinds of buildings—types of shops, banks, offices and public buildings—in a town. The procession of the seasons and the recording of weather have long been points of interest in primary schools. The promotion of more accurate means of expression takes time—time to observe, to handle, to collect, to ask questions, to draw out distinctions, to record in paintings, models, writing, or orally on tape. And as children gain precision in distinguishing so

11

they learn to be more precise in counting, measuring and describing. 'Our road has a lot of traffic' is later more precisely stated as 'in half-an-hour we counted 47 cars, 18 lorries, 6 buses, 9 vans, 4 tankers, 8 motor-cycles and 22 bicycles passing the school gate'. A histogram recording this information provides a handy means of comparison for juniors who may choose to compare traffic flow at different periods in the day. Such an exercise may lead on to comparing traffic flows in different directions which, in turn, develops into the beginnings of interpreting the rhythm of traffic in a town. This, in many cases, is an index of the rhythm of economic life as people move to and from their places of work or the shops, though for most areas such an analysis is more appropriately done at the secondary stage. Weather, at first recorded in pictures or short phrases, may later be quoted in measured temperatures and rainfall with comments on wind direction and clouds. Repeated observations permit comparisons; graphs begin to find a place; and later older juniors may relate temperatures to wind directions and rainfall to cloud types. Soils may first be investigated by 'feel' for stickiness or dryness; later the particles and vegetable content may be studied with a hand lens; later the top horizon—usually darker—may be measured and compared with the lower horizon. The same principles may be applied to many aspects of local study, for example to farms, houses and other buildings, and roads. The trend from simple to more detailed observation and vocabulary, from simple to more precise statements, from facts to relationships, are all part of the process of growing up in thinking. Similarly the description of a single process, as on a farm, or the observed flow of a stream may be replaced by describing a sequence of operations or changes. In the case of a stream observed over a period of time the older children begin to describe why changes take place —why the water is sometimes deep and sometimes shallow, at one time muddy and at another time clear.

Organisation
It has already been suggested that the teacher should be concerned with the whole environment and not only with what may loosely be called geography. The number of primary schools that treat geography as a separate subject has steadily diminished; instead a generic term such as social studies, or environmental studies or topic studies embraces a range of learning which for most children, and quite properly, has not yet become differentiated into the distinctive areas and modes of knowing which are characteristic of the traditional subjects. The unfettered freedom which children enjoy in pursuing their own investigations and interests produces work of extraordinary vitality, particularly when the teacher has prepared the groundwork, has afforded time for each experience to be understood

and to bring forth its own potential for further development, and has provided the facilities for the children to continue with this development. Nowhere is this more apparent than in the study of the local environment where science, history, art, geography and language may intermingle in rich combination.[1]

There are, however, pitfalls which, with a little thought, can be avoided. Unless the teacher keeps a careful eye on the balance of the programme he may neglect, or completely omit, the vocabulary and understandings which are an essential foundation to later learning. This is more likely to happen in the elements that contribute to science, history and geography than to art, mathematics and language. Secondly, in a programme of undifferentiated learning it is particularly necessary to ensure that the children's work is sufficiently progressive in its intellectual quality; enrichment of vocabulary, increasing precision of expression and the beginnings of reasoning will not happen by accident and need to be consciously encouraged. Thirdly, the teacher should not be surprised if children sometimes pursue enquiries which are to all intents scientific, historical or geographical. The more mature may well begin to think in terms of separate subjects quite naturally because they are capable of discarding factors which disturb their main purpose. Such children should not be discouraged; at the same time others should not be prematurely forced into the more logical and orderly processes of thinking which this kind of work demands.

General Aids
Even at the primary stage geography cannot be confined to a consideration of the local environment, and, perhaps, for those more fortunate schools, to one or two contrasting environments which are visited with a view to widening the range of direct study. Windows on the world are opened in a variety of ways. Sound radio and television programmes devised for younger and older children afford accuracy of detail and authenticity of atmosphere which the teacher would find it difficult to match. They are, moreover, backed by considerable research on the part of those responsible for their production, including consumer research which enables the BBC and ITV authorities to keep in touch with the schools and their needs. For the busy teacher notes of guidance provide useful background material, and pupils' pamphlets contain pictures and other information. In the main broadcast lessons afford a rich source of learning material which the teacher needs to exploit and consolidate if full

---

[1] For a more detailed treatment of this and other themes, see *Geography in Primary Schools*. Geographical Association: 1970.

value is to be gained from them. As with other forms of learning time must be taken to discover what the impact has been on the children. For some the content may require clarification, the words used may bear repetition and discussion, the events, processes or descriptions may merit pictorial or written records, which themselves reveal the depth of response achieved. For others the broadcast lesson may be a jumping-off ground, a stimulus to further enquiry in atlases and books. In the same class the teacher may need to provide opportunities for a variety of reactions according to the differing degrees of comprehension and stages of maturity among the children. Nothing is less likely to reap the full potential harvest of these lessons than a standard follow-up task which all the children carry out regardless of their abilities and interests. Freed from the shackles of rigid timetables far greater use of broadcast lessons is now possible to the teacher who is looking for fresh materials on which to base classroom activities. Ciné film and film-strips may also have strong visual appeal. It is, perhaps, worth repeating that, particularly with young children, no teacher can be sure that the pictures shown will have the same effects on all; many children require help to see what a picture is designed to portray, and the skill of 'reading' pictures may continue to call for assistance by the teacher right through the primary and secondary school. Indeed this skill is now tested at its more refined level by many examining boards in their geography examinations.

Some of the recent work which is being tried in junior schools involving mathematics and role-playing games deserves the attention of teachers interested in promoting new ways of learning. One of the principles lying behind this work, which will receive the approval of teachers, is that the children actually carry out operations within a set of rules and so learn by doing. The rules are based on general knowledge about the topic in question. Thus if a group of children 'manage' a farm for several hypothetical years they decide what crops to grow and in which fields within certain restrictions which actually apply to the farmer. When they calculate their profits they will understand the need for variety in the production on a farm where different kinds of weather may favour some crops and be less favourable to others. They will learn why some fields cannot be ploughed as, for example, a permanent pasture field in a valley bottom with a high watertable or liability to floods. Similarly games can be constructed for building a railway or port, for establishing a factory, for building a shopping centre. In each case the rules are arranged to suit the level of understanding of the children and to introduce basic knowledge. As far as geography is concerned these ideas are, as yet, in their infancy, but they are likely to provide a fruitful source of experiment and creative thinking for teachers and children.[2]

Books

Few people know better than experienced teachers of infants and young juniors the importance that children attach to their parents, homes and friends and their immediate day-to-day affairs. These form the real and realistic bases of young children's judgments and of their appreciation of other people, social practices and human situations. Against these, comparisons are made, often subconsciously. Books about children and families in other lands have, therefore, a special appeal to young children. Presentation by teachers of the ways of life of peoples of many lands requires not only up-to-date knowledge of social and economic developments and the changes they bring but also skilled and sympathetic reference to the many differences that exist in the outlooks, cultures and practices of geographically separated societies. Some simplification is unavoidable but the perpetuation of impressions of conditions of life which are no longer supported by geographical or sociological facts is scarcely to be excused. For the range of attractive material is wide and the possibility of obtaining well produced story books illustrated by good photography or delightful line or coloured drawings is open to most schools. Geography is enriched by using books by foreign authors. Among recent publications are lighthearted, whimsical and even funny books from France, Iran, Holland, the Balkans, Norway, Japan, Italy, Switzerland and India, 'The Nock Family Circus' is concerned with life in a real Swiss travelling circus: 'Children of the North Lights' is a beautifully drawn story of the Lapland year; 'Gennorino' contains lovely pictures of Italian seaside and town; 'Minou' is unmistakably French; 'Travelling and Tippety' shows excellent pictures of the Balkan countryside, architecture and costumes, as toys seeking a mender travel through the land; Paravathi Thampi's 'Geata and the Village School'—a story of a small girl in a present-day Indian village told simply for young children—is not a tale of improbable adventure but one of a child fearing changes in her immediate environment.

Adventure has been the driving force that impels many good stories. Some, like the American 'Komantica', do not baulk at realism, and the much acclaimed 'Shifta' by Forbes Watson depicts the harsh Somaliland countryside through the eyes of a native in a way that conveys its beauty. Continental writers have offered new fare in

[2] See Walford: *Games in Geography*. Longmans 1969 and Cole and Beynon: *New Ways in Geography*. Blackwell 1968.

translations of foreign books. Names like R. Crillot, A. Rutgens, Van der Loeff, Meindert de Jong, Paul Berna and Manfred Michael are to be found in the catalogues of authors in many class-and school-libraries. A room equipped with books of the kinds mentioned here is a storehouse of geographical experiences which may be left to carry their own messages or used by a teacher, much as he might use a series of broadcast lessons, to stimulate questions, discussion and further enquiry.

There are, in addition, books written specifically for younger children to convey information—about people, rivers, animals, railways, towns and farms, to mention a few of the topics that teachers would find valuable in extending geographical knowledge and interest. Among these special mention may be made of publications of the Association of Agriculture which deal with real farms at home and abroad and which, in many cases, are kept up-to-date by reports, often in narrative form, written by the farmer. Some of them are more suitable for secondary rather than primary schools, but there is material produced specially for younger children. On almost any topic that a teacher could name as having geographical implications books for the young reader have increasingly been promoted by publishers. A widely ranging library of such works, easily accessible for occasional browsing and more protracted reading, affords both a wealth of inspiration for fresh discovery and exploration and a means of finding answers to questions that child or teacher may pose. These two quite separate purposes need to be appreciated by the teacher if full value is to be gained from the class library. Not only are books sometimes to be enjoyed and allowed to convey pleasure and satisfaction without interference, but they are also tools to be used.

Within any single primary school a book on Lapland depicting the life of a group of people in photographs with brief captions possesses a diversity of uses. Some children may stare uncomprehendingly at the pictorial record; they have no standards of reference and no words to interpret the reindeer with their branching horns, the outlandish mode of dress of the people and their implements, the patchwork of snow and verdure with stunted birch growing on scattered sites. Such children need unhurried conversation with a sympathetic teacher if they are to gain any insight into a land and a way of life so completely alien to their own. For them the questions 'Where?' and 'What is it like?' may be satisfactorily answered in terms of a place which is far away, which has long cold winters and summers too short and cool to grow crops, a land where very few ~ople live. Some children may ask for no help; they read the book ~ver to cover revelling in the magic of the new world that is revealed and, returning to it to savour its delights again. When a book of this kind establishes itself as a favourite in a class or group the teacher may decide that this is the time to take the initiative and suggest other ways in which the children may discover more about the Lapps, using a well written textbook or other reference books which are available. In this way a topic on people who live in cold lands may be developed and the globe and maps may be consulted. The question of place thus becomes more precisely defined in a universal frame of reference which becomes increasingly familiar with use; the relationship between cold areas and northerly latitudes (or high altitudes) begins to emerge, leading to the concept of subpolar and high altitude climates. But the same book may have yet another use for children whose reading has made them inquisitive about people living in inhospitable climates. They may turn to the book to enlarge their knowledge and fill in details, scanning every picture with analytical eyes, looking for every clue which will help them to understand more of the way of life of the people and how it is adjusted to a harsh environment, seeking answers to questions about the education of the children, medical care and the trade which will provide money for purchasing goods that cannot be produced locally. One of the greatest rewards for the teacher is that work of this kind occasionally takes him beyond his own immediate resources to the point where he can enjoy learning with the children.

Progression
Certain ideas are implicit in the foregoing sections which suggest a mode of progression in geographical teaching in the primary school. The first is that the size of the unit studied should initially be very small, whether it be a single person or group, an aspect of a farm, a group of shops, a short piece of road, a patch of woodland, or an element of weather. It is only when a child has built up a familiarity with a large number of small elements that he can begin to understand situations involving several elements, or to approach the 'sample study', or more accurately the 'case study'—an intimate and realistic presentation of a small unit seen in its many facets and calling for some understanding of the relationships that exist among them. The case study of an irrigated farm in an arid area, for example, requires some appreciation of the facts that some places have little or no rain, that crops require moisture, that water can be conveyed in channels or pipes from rivers or reservoirs, that people develop special ways of managing a difficult environment, and that foodstuffs which may be quite different from those known to the child may be a staple diet for another people. But these facts are woven into a texture in which the threads of climate, farming practice, the techniques of water management and types of crops are inter-related.

In such a study the children will ask why? as well as how? Sample studies of this kind involving small communities or areas afford opportunities for reasoning at an uncomplicated level without the complexities that arise when larger units or areas are studied. Too often the study of large areas like the Pampas, or of whole countries like Norway, with younger children has been achieved by over-simplification and generalisation which distorts the truth. Topics on this scale are best left to a later stage; and for some pupils they may occur in the primary school while for others they may most profitably be left to the secondary school. Secondly the idea of place, too, takes time to establish. A young junior may enjoy seeing or making a large-scale plan of his own neighbourhood and through using it may begin to understand how a two-dimensional representation of a piece of the earth's surface can be recorded in this way. A finer appreciation of scale is, however, a later development, and though the regular use of a globe as a model, and later, of small-scale maps of Britain or the Continents may result in familiarity and may help children towards an understanding of relative positions, a true appreciation of the distances and sizes involved is slow to emerge. Thirdly concepts involving general ideas about climate, vegetation, landscape features and economic activity may be within the grasp of some older juniors, but for many, if they are presented too early, they result in the meaningless use of words and phrases which ultimately produce confusion of thought.

Assessment

To provide suitable materials and situations for learning is but one aspect of the teacher's job. He must be constantly assessing the results of the learning process as revealed by children's reactions in their conversation and records. Children do not conform to a common mould at eight, or nine, or ten years of age. While some are quick to comprehend the relationships between climate and farming others are still learning to recognise and name the animals, crops and machines used on a farm, or to appreciate the separate elements that make up weather. While some can refer to an atlas and use a scale others are still unaware of the names of the major land and sea masses represented on the globe. While some can classify, record, and describe the main public buildings and shops in a small town centre others have not yet learned to distinguish the types of shops. If the tasks that children are expected to do are not related to their stage of understanding, frustration and boredom can follow. Not only should the teacher have clear ideas about the purposes of his geographical teaching, but he must be prepared to adapt the work so that all children have a sense of achievement. The secondary school cannot build successfully on a foundation of failure, lack of understanding, or underachievement which breeds indifference. Nor should it turn its back on what has gone before and ignore the work of the primary school. For geography, as for other areas of learning, the problems of transition from primary to secondary school can be eased if the children have a sense of continuity. Teachers in primary and secondary schools have much to learn from one another, and time spent in consultation about programmes of work, resources for learning, methods of teaching and the progress made by the children individually or in groups, will not be wasted.

What can the primary school expect of its leavers in terms of geographical experience? There is certainly no single standard of knowledge and skill which is appropriate to all, but it would not be unreasonable to expect that, with few exceptions:

(a) they would have examined at first hand selected features of their own local environment—its weather, its surface features both natural and man-made, and something of the economic activity of its inhabitants;

(b) they would have had encouragement and opportunity to get to know something of contrasting and comparable small environments in Britain and abroad and had come to realise that the world contains great variety in the conditions under which people live and the ways in which they respond to these conditions;

(c) they would be able to make records, with varying degrees of precision, in pictures, models, maps, diagrams, graphs and writing;

(d) they would be familiar with the globe and with atlas maps and would be able to distinguish surface features such as high land, rivers, countries and cities;

(e) they had used, and were interested in, pictures and books as sources of learning about their own and other countries;

(f) they were already acquainted with large-scale maps of their own neighbourhood and, possibly, one or two other areas which they had visited;

(g) they were accustomed to the idea of location by means of direction and distance.

In addition abler boys and girls may well have advanced to the stage at which they analyse in a more penetrating way the geographical material which they study in the field or the classroom and are seeking to explain the relationships that exist between one phenomenon and another, for example, the differences in land use between highland and lowland Britain, the functions of towns with respect to their surrounding areas, or the way in which history still influences the character of a town or countryside or road system. Such children may well have perceived some of the patterns of distribution and location that are to be seen on the landscape and in maps, but this is a stage to which most children will not aspire until their minds are more mature.

The effect of the Middle School
There are few Middle Schools in existence, and those have not yet had a long enough life to establish their distinctive patterns of organisation and education. Any discussion which concerns them must therefore be somewhat theoretical and exploratory. During their life in the Middle School many children will progress in their mode of learning towards more consistent logical thinking; this is an important transitional period in their development.[3] While the younger children may spend much of their day under the guidance of one or two teachers many of the older will need to have access to teachers with specialist knowledge in certain fields. For some subjects setting across an age group may be needed, but the organisational difficulties would undoubtedly limit the amount of setting that could be sustained. Geography is not likely to be among the subjects which are setted. The well established practice in Primary Schools of adjusting work to individual interests and capacities, if extended to the older children in Middle Schools, is likely to be an advance on practice in many Secondary Schools where class exercises are still the rule rather than the exception. Indeed, where classes of mixed ability are present then group-work, adjusted to the abilities of children, will be essential if the abler are not to be forced into a programme of underachievement or their slower classmates confronted with ideas beyond their present stage of comprehension and tasks which inevitably subject them to failure.

Staffing
Every Middle School will need the services of at least one teacher well versed in modern geography and its teaching. He should keep in touch with literature on the subject, especially that sponsored by institutions such as the Schools Council and the Geographical Association, and should be informed about current and proposed broadcast lessons of the BBC and ITV authorities. His colleagues should be able to turn to him for advice on equipment, visual aids, books of all kinds, and schemes of work; the children should be able to turn to him when they require help which is beyond the resources of other members of the staff. He should, wherever possible, maintain contact with geography teachers in the Secondary School, to which

---

[3] See *Towards The Middle School*. HMSO, 1970.

the boys and girls will ultimately be transferred. In addition to his work as a consultant and leader in geography, he will undoubtedly be involved in other subjects, and for teaching them he may well expect to receive the sort of guidance which he gives for geography. In smaller schools he may be asked to act as a consultant in two subjects; such an assignment may make heavy demands on him, but combinations of geography with history or science or mathematics may prove to have a good deal of common ground. Teachers who have graduated in combined studies such as social studies, environmental studies and area studies should find that their training has particular relevance to the needs of Middle Schools.

The Programme

One of the benefits that the Middle School will inherit from the Primary School is the greater flexibility in the management of time which is possible. Geography may no longer be tied to two or three lessons distributed through the week with the attendant disadvantages of discontinuity—a short period of revision at the beginning of each lesson to revive the memory or interest, the hasty attempt to reach a suitable conclusion as the clock moves on, the parcelling out of geography in small units designed to fit a period of thirty or forty minutes or the taking out and putting away of maps, books and equipment as one subject succeeds another. Continuous periods of study in a single week, even though they occur only four or five times in a term, are more likely to lead to effective work by the children than the equivalent amount of time spread thinly in weekly allocations throughout the term. They also ease the teacher's burdens of preparation and development of the theme in hand, and of devising a suitable range of tasks to match the varying capacities of the children.

Geographical experience may take on four quite different forms:

(a) It may rise incidentally and briefly at any time of the day.
(b) It may occur in the extended study of a topic or theme which embraces elements of several traditional subject areas.
(c) It may occupy the central place in a topic in which other elements are subsidiary but by no means unimportant.
(d) It may to all intents and purposes be straightforward geography.

Each of these categories merits some elaboration:

(a) Every teacher is familiar with the phenomenon of the 'incidental question'. How far did the Israelites have to go to escape from the Egyptians? Why were they short of water? Why is that music called

C

'Finlandia'? Where does rubber come from? Why do we call this a 'jungle gym'? Happy the teacher who can, from a well-furnished mind or a well-furnished classroom, provide satisfactory answers to the unpredictable flow of questions. But happier still the teacher who perceives when an incidental question has, by one means or another, become a focus of intense interest that sets a group on a course of enquiry leading to the extended exploration of a topic.

(b) Some topics arise, then, unexpectedly, and depend for their successful pursuit on the adaptability of the teacher to unforeseen demands and the availability of suitable resources for learning. More commonly the teacher is alerted to the possibilities of the trends that children's enquiries may follow. Experience of outdoor visits, of well-loved stories or of the abiding interest of younger children in the familiar objects and events in their lives makes it possible to predict the kinds of enquiries that will arise and the ways in which they may be canalised. It is also important that the teacher should, particularly with older children, take the initiative in introducing topics for study, chosen because they deal with important areas of knowledge and require the acquisition of skills for which the children are deemed to be ready. The choice and development of topics should take account of the great difference that exists between the modes of learning of younger and older pupils. To young children almost nothing is trivial; the teacher who can follow their interests and enthusiasms, helping them individually or in small groups to observe more closely, to communicate about their experiences and to find answers to their questions can generally be satisfied that the children are working with purpose and profit. The same cannot be said to apply universally to older children, some of whom, without guidance, may spend long periods of time on repetitive activities with no progression in knowledge or understanding. As topics of greater complexity are explored the teacher has a greater responsibility to offer direction to the work in hand.

Any familiar subject, such as a street, a bridge, houses, clothing, motor vehicles, water, trees or weather, is capable of being studied in an infinite variety of ways. Let us take the example of clothing; some mathematical work might be done on standard sizes of garments, sizes of shoes worn by children in a class, the weights of different materials, costings, and the ways in which patterns are made up for dresses and coats; historically the topic is rich with possibilities among which may be mentioned changes in dress through historical times, related to the conditions of life and available resources, the silk trade, village crafts, the wool trade, the early woollen industry and the growth of the textile industries of the 18th and 19th Centuries; a great deal of work in art and craft might well arise from historical

and contemporary studies of clothing; scientific studies might be
concerned with the nature of the yarn and weaving methods in
woollens, cottons and man-made fibres, with testing for insulation,
strength, wear, shrinkage, and washing and drying properties; the
geographical aspects might include sources of raw materials, factories
and manufacturing areas, and the different modes of dress, of
different peoples, the materials used and the ways in which clothing
is associated with climates, available materials and stages of economic development. Some of the elements in this by no means exhaustive list would be suitable for abler or older children and some
for younger or less able. How does the teacher ensure that over a
period of time, for example a year, due weight is given to each area
of the curriculum (or subject) which is subsumed under a general
title such as 'topic studies'? It is not uncommon to find that for one
reason or another the work carried out by children has a strong bias
towards historical or geographical or scientific studies. Carried to
extreme this may mean that the children can go for long periods
during which some subject areas are completely neglected. It is,
therefore, important that the teacher should retain some control over
the content of the work, and this can be done by keeping records of
the sort of activities carried out by (a) the class, (b) groups and (c)
individuals. Thus, to concentrate on geography, the teacher's record
of the project on clothing, carried out by the children of ten or eleven
years of age, might include the following section.

Geographical:
1. Case studies on sheep farms:

Group (a) (children named)	North Wales
(b)	Tweed Basin
(c)	Falkland Islands
(d)	Australia
(e)	South Africa

Talks given to class by each group; farms located on maps of
Britain and World, and journeys from home discussed. Class-map
made to show journeys to each farm and stopping places en route
to the distant places, by air and sea routes.

2. Picture collections and written descriptive accounts of clothing
worn in:

Group (a)	Russia
(b)	India
(c)	Spain
(d)	Nigeria
(e)	Japan

Location of places featured in pictures shown on world map. Discussion by class on differences between countries. The top group (children named) were given the task of finding out about the climates of the countries to see whether the clothing reflected differences. They made their first climate graphs:—for Moscow, Bombay, Madrid, Lagos, Yokohama.

Note for future reference: Russia proved too complicated because of great variations in climate. The contrasts between modern and traditional dress in Japan aroused great interest; a study of Japan would probably be successful.

Records of this kind are necessary if the teacher is to organise topic studies purposefully. It may well be that the next set of studies will include no geography of any substance, but this will not matter if, over a period of a term or half a year, geography occupies a reasonable place in the range of activities and includes not only the gathering of new knowledge but also the practice of basic skills like locating places on maps, using information on maps to find distances, and drawing climatic graphs. From time to time the teacher needs to examine his records to see if each subject area is satisfactorily represented.

(c) One of the results of trying to keep a balance across the range of activities in 'projects' is that the teacher may occasionally consider that not enough geography is emerging from the general topic studies. In such a case he refers to his past records and may decide to stimulate an interest in an essentially geographical topic. For example the previously quoted section of a teacher's record suggests that some aspects of Japan might prove interesting. This may be introduced to a whole class by the teacher, possibly using a cine film, or film strip, or a broadcast lesson; there might, too, be a special display of pictures and books on Japan. What follows the general introduction would depend on the age and ability of the children. At an elementary stage there could be vignettes of life in Japan—a coastal village with fishing and the cultivation of small plots of rice and vegetables as the main economic activity, tea and rice-growing in Southern Japan, traditional Japanese dress and houses and their modern counterparts, the life of a worker in a silk factory at Osaka, pilgrims and tourists on Fujiyama, a paper mill in Hokkaido. Other children might be examining atlas maps, noting the variations in climate from North to South, establishing an understanding of the relationships between physical features and settlement, explaining the importance of hydro-electric power, of the great fishing fleets, and of the growth of modern industry. This may well be typical of the range of geographical work that could be attempted in a mixed ability class of twelve-year-olds. But some of the work might move naturally into the recent history of Japan, or the Samurai tradition, or Japanese painting, prints and lacquer-ware. Thus while the project would have a firm geographical core it would not prohibit children from following interesting side-tracks.

When individuals and groups are, in this way, pursuing different kinds of work associated with a common theme it is important that some sharing of experience should take place towards the end of the exercise. It calls for a great deal of skill on the part of the teacher to bring various pieces of work of this kind into some kind of order, to act as a chairman encouraging children to explain to others what they have learned, interpreting expositions which need clarifying and weaving together the many strands into a recognisable fabric.

(d) As the children grow older some of them may enter Piaget's stage of 'formal operations' in the upper classes of the Middle School. In practice this means that they are capable of deductive and inductive thinking, are able to arrive at generalised statements and can be made aware of the strengths and weaknesses of simple generalisations. Such children may wish to undertake studies that belong essentially to recognisable subjects (in the traditional sense) and they should be given every encouragement to do so. This does not mean that they will revert to two or three lessons of geography per week. In the same class there will possibly be other children who are still working at an intellectually less mature level. It is more than likely that some subjects will have to be done in a time-table framework designed for 'topic studies'. This is no bad thing for the boy or girl studying subjects such as history, geography or science. As has been suggested earlier discontinuous but generous blocks of time may be more profitable than a similar amount of time in small weekly rations.

At this stage children should be arriving at general concepts by empirical studies of particular situations and using these concepts to interpret similar situations. Simple hypotheses may be arrived at and tested in the field or in studies of distant areas provided that the data is not too complex. For example a study of the Equatorial Forest belt of Africa in which the natural vegetation is linked with temperature and rainfall regimes may suggest some general ideas about climate and vegetation. Given climatic maps for tropical South America it is possible to suggest the extent of Equatorial Forest in that continent. Groups of pupils may work together on such an exercise to produce a theoretical map which may be tested against a map of natural vegetation. Discrepancies between the theoretical map and a real map need explanation. Or, to choose an example of field work, pupils who already have learned about soil horizons and the widening of river valleys by sub-aerial denudation may deduce that, since soil-wash on slopes tends to erode the 'A' horizon then a theoretical model of the variations in thickness of the 'A' horizon across a small valley at X, Y, and Z would be as follows:

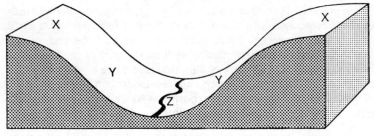

Figure 1.

At X — 'normal' depth—little erosion.
At Y — less than normal depth—due to surface erosion.
At Z — more than normal depth—due to downwash.

This is a theory that can be tested simply by digging a number of small soil-pits. The class may also wish to test a theory that, where the slop is variable the depth of the 'A' horizon diminishes as the slope increases. Or again after examining large-scale maps of their home town the pupils may mark convergence points as the places of slowest traffic flow. Traffic counts taken at suitable places near to, and distant from, the convergence points, may prove or disprove the theory; in the latter case it may lead to further studies of traffic generation and flow—important points in local planning. The value of work of this kind is that the pupils apply knowledge of facts and relationships to the solution of real problems and that the solutions themselves often generate further learning. The pupils are actively engaged in pursuing knowledge and not passive recipients.

The foregoing paragraph has been concerned with one method of learning. The question of content still remains to be dealt with. For younger children the earlier section on the primary school offers some guidance. As for the upper end of the Middle School it may be useful to attempt to describe in broad terms the kinds of geography with which our average pupil should be familiar if he is to undertake the work of the Secondary School with any confidence. The work should certainly have moved well beyond the targets set for the Primary School in the last chapter. Many children should:

(a) in the case of medium and large scale maps know most of the common symbols, be able to follow a simple route on roads and lanes, be able to recognise a number of contour forms such as spurs, hills and steep slopes, and be able to scale off distances.

(b) be thoroughly familiar, through using maps, with the main features of relief of the continents and Britain and be able to describe distributions of temperature, rainfall, vegetation and population from uncomplicated maps which use isopleths and colours to show variations.

(c) be aware that the earth's surface is subject to forces of denudation operating upon a variety of land forms and that denudation is accompanied by deposition; they should, wherever possible, have made first-hand studies of some aspects of these processes and of the vegetation and soil mantle that overlies the harder rocks in most areas.

(d) be able to collect and record climatic data—temperature, rainfall, wind direction and main cloud types.

(e) have a good grasp of the pattern of distribution of some of the main vegetation zones with their associated climates, particularly the equatorial forests, savannas, hot deserts, the temperate deciduous forests, the temperate grasslands and the cold coniferous forest belts; the more complex transitional and monsoonal regions can be left until later.

(f) have made in the fields of human geography a number of studies of farming and know that animals and crops vary according to climate and the markets, and be aware that the great differences in standards of living among the nations are associated with industrial development and trade, as well as with the tools that man has at his disposal.

(g) have learned through urban studies to recognise functional zones—residential, industrial and commercial—where they are clearly defined.

(h) have included in their studies of other environments a number of countries at different stages of development dealt with in some depth to show how physical features, climate, natural resources and human response vary from one place to another.

Finally they should have learned much of their geography through using sources of information—maps of many kinds, pictures, statistics, graphs, diagrams (including annotated transect diagrams), sketchmaps, and written accounts—for pupils who pass into the upper school with no experience of using the tools of learning are severely handicapped.

It may be fitting to close this section by emphasising the importance of well kept and co-ordinated records of work. In a school where geography is taught in accordance with a carefully planned scheme of work the stages of development in vocabulary, skills, relationships and knowledge follow a prearranged order which is based on experience. When, however, geography is taught for a good deal of the time in association with other subjects it is more difficult to ensure (a) that a reasonable share of time is given to geographical experience (b) that unprofitable repetition is avoided and (c) that progression takes place. The purpose of records of work is to take over some of the functions of a scheme of work. As children grow older it is not enough to allow one topic to follow another without regard to the content as it affects the subject areas. Sometimes general topics serve as admirable vehicles for teaching geography at an appropriate level; sometimes it may be necessary for the teacher to introduce topics which are mainly or wholly geographical. The record of work must therefore be kept and matched against a general model of the levels of geography that seem to be suitable at each stage of the school. Such a model may take the form of a list of skills and types of studies; it must, however, take into account the wide range of ability that may exist in a class and should not be planned in terms of chronological age. Both the model and the record of work should be concerned with the general stages of development which have been indicated in earlier pages. Records should be available for use by geography teachers in the Secondary School; indeed consultation between teachers in both schools is essential to ensure continuity in the programmes of work.

Equipment

Among younger children much of the geographical teaching will take place in the classroom work area which is used for many other activities. The immediate availability of books of many kinds, materials for measuring, making models, painting and drawing, and space for mounting and examining collections of objects form a favourable setting in which children can pursue investigations of many kinds. While older children will need more advanced and specialised aids the amount of geography taught would not justify setting up a special geography room. Geography could be well served if the teaching aids which it needs were brought together in a single teaching room, or in two adjacent rooms, with an associated work-space into which work could overflow on occasions. Some of the equipment used in mathematics and science would also be needed for geography, for example instruments for measuring, weighing, making simple maps, making weather observations, and studying soils, fossils and rocks. With science, history and English geography shares a common interest in literature, books of reference and visual aids and with making various kinds of records—graphical, diagrammatic, written and solid models. There are, too, materials which are special to geography. Globes and wall-maps are needed in every room where geography is taught and they should be constantly used. There should, too, be a variety of atlases, a small collection of large-scale maps ranging from 50 inches to the mile to the quarter-inch scale (or their new metricated counterparts) for areas which are studied in some detail, well catalogued collections of pictures for wall-display and projection, specimens of objects and materials for children to handle and examine, and three-dimensional models which are often associated with physical and mathematical geography. For older children shared tables are suitable, and flat-topped surfaces in the form of side-benches or tables are needed for many purposes. One of the great advantages of a more integrated approach to teaching is that the books that children and teachers require will often be close at hand in the classroom or work area. The kinds of books that a teacher chooses should reflect his views of the content of the course, which will tend to vary according to the locality and the teacher. The bias that comes through living in a great port or a farming area, or from a teacher's interest in weather studies or Africa, can be expected to have some influence on the choice of books in the library. But all Middle Schools will need a good collection of books about Britain and foreign lands, including many that give intimate pictures about small areas such as have been mentioned earlier in the section on the Primary School. In addition there should be books, including text-books, of a more formal nature suitable for the older and more mature boys and girls who are ready for a closely reasoned treatment of regions, countries and general topics.

4

Older Pupils

In the immediate post-war years most geography teachers in Grammar Schools, working towards syllabuses for the first examination, attempted in a five-year course to combine a study of map-reading and elementary physical and mathematical geography with regional surveys designed to 'cover the world' though the amount of detail included in regional studies tended to vary from one region or continent to another. In Modern Schools, where an earlier leaving-age prevailed, various forms of shortened 'world coverage' were attempted, and physical and mathematical geography tended to occupy a much smaller place in the schemes of work; experiments in social studies, environmental studies and projects which did not conform tidily to traditional subject areas were also afoot. The distinction between the academic courses of the Grammar School and the non-academic courses of the Modern was widely accepted. In academic courses, and to some extent in non-academic courses, there ran a strong thread of determinism or probabilism which attempted to interpret human activity in terms of physical geography, regardless of the extent to which technological, economic, political and social forces were at work. An overemphasis on the influence of the relatively unchanging factors of physical geography tended to result in a static picture of human societies which was out of harmony with the facts of a rapidly changing world. Moreover the attempt to deal with so much material often led to generalisations and superficiality that left pupils with a skeleton of knowledge rather than an understanding of a living pulsating world. Many teachers of geography, concerned at the courses which their subject was taking, were beginning to re-appraise the content of syllabuses and methods of teaching.

There was a growing realisation that no hard and fast line existed between pupils admitted to Grammar and Modern schools. Side by side with the idea of a continuum of ability across the secondary schools grew an awareness that the distinction between primary and secondary schools was not clear-cut; no longer was it evident that all pupils were ready to move at the same time from a primary education which laid a general foundation of geographical experience to a secondary education in which a logical and orderly systematising of knowledge was appropriate. The continuum of ability was seen to exist both vertically and horizontally. Lastly the increasing tendency to operate systems of options in the curriculum meant that many pupils might drop the serious study of geography at fourteen years of age— and in a small proportion of schools even earlier. Thus certain assumptions upon which geography teaching had been based, namely the length of the secondary school course and the abilities of pupils, were no longer regarded as valid. In addition there are those who believe that geography may, for at least some pupils, be more profitably taught in combination with other subjects in, for example, a humanities course or as part of social studies or environmental studies

How are teachers of geography reacting to the changing circumstances in which their role is played? It is possible to discern a number of distinctive trends. In the first place there is a greater willingness to select certain topics or themes from the vast geographical repertoire and to concentrate attention on them; and a policy of selection has, as its corollary a policy of rejection. Secondly greater emphasis is being placed on training pupils to identify and handle the kinds of evidence that geographers use in the field and the classroom. Thirdly they are more concerned than formerly with helping their pupils to arrive at general concepts instead of relying upon memorising isolated facts. And lastly they are seeking ways of applying geographical skills and concepts to an understanding of problems which in one way or another impinge on the lives of the pupils. Each of these themes is examined in greater detail in succeeding sections and chapters.

Selection

At the outset a distinction must be drawn between courses of work in geography which in the later stages of secondary education are concerned with preparing pupils for examinations for the General Certificate of Education, over which any individual teacher's control may be slight, and courses which are not subject to such external pressures. As far as geography is concerned the proportion of pupils affected by such examinations at the age of sixteen represents about one-quarter of an age group, while those going on to Advanced level are much fewer in number. For these pupils a stage is reached, usually in the fourth year of the secondary school, when the examination syllabus dominates the course. This is not to suggest that preparation for the Ordinary and Advanced level examinations for the General Certificate of Education leaves no margin of choice to the teacher, or that the examination syllabuses are inflexibly managed. A comparative study of syllabuses and examination papers over the last fifteen years shows that a wider choice of regional studies has become available, that questions which require evidence of a candidate's ability to handle and interpret a variety of data have increased, and that problems concerning world poverty and development regularly appear,[1] to mention a few of the changes that have taken place.

Nevertheless an examination designed to serve a large number of schools and to do justice to a wide range of teacher opinion cannot but contain an element of constraint for individual schools. No such constraint need be applied to the large majority of pupils in schools—the whole of the lower school and the majority in the upper who do not prepare for the General Certificate in geography. For pupils aiming at the Certificate of Secondary Education it is within the power of each school to make its own Mode III syllabus. Few teachers avail themselves of the opportunity to submit their own syllabuses for the General Certificate of Education.

Faced with a large degree of freedom it is not surprising that many teachers are choosing those areas of geography which they deem to be most useful to their pupils in helping them to understand the world in which they live. It does not follow that a choice of geographical studies based on a criterion of usefulness need be any less demanding intellectually than one based on regional and systematic studies cast in a traditional mould. Usefulness is generally conceived as operating at three levels—the home region, Britain, and the world beyond, though it is clear that they cannot and should not be regarded in isolation. It is in the home region that boys and girls may meet at first-hand the complexities of a highly organised and economically advanced society; here it is that they meet a world in which physical features, climate, soils and other natural resources, history, social customs, economics and the policies of local and national governments all combine to give its existing appearance and character; and here they may study at first hand forces of change which are shaping the future not only of their own country but also in greater or lesser degree countries all over the world. It is here that the foundation of vocabulary and simple relationships laid in the primary school can be extended by direct contact to more sophisticated terminologies and relationships. At first the choice of topics for study will be limited in their scope, for example a comparison of two shopping centres, two or three farms and their similarities and differences, the siting of factories, traffic surveys and the like. But as

---

[1] See *Impact '69*. Published by the Voluntary Committee on Overseas Aid and Development.

the pupils grow older general concepts will emerge. Farming will be seen not only in terms of management of land but also in its relationships to markets, government subsidies and the competition exerted by imports. The difference between large scale industries subject to international competition and those light industries which are frequently orientated to the home market will emerge. Traffic surveys lead to an analysis of road networks and shopping centres to the structure, functions and morphology of urban areas and to the concept of central places. Planning, a subject in which all future citizens ought to be informed, will be seen in a real context of existing or anticipated problems such as road congestion, poor housing, water supply, sewage disposal, recreational needs and conservation. Each home region studied in this way will provide parallels by which other regions in Britain and abroad may be studied. The lowland farming areas of Britain, the older industrial areas, the vigorously expanding 'new' industrial areas, the tourist areas, and the highland and marginal farming areas have much in common with their counterparts in Western Europe and parts of North America. General ideas that emerge from a well-planned course of study on the home region can throw light on areas far removed from it.

The geography of Britain can be approached in a number of ways. For abler pupils the distribution of highland and lowland areas and of the significant climatic variations that exist may prove a useful framework within which regional studies may be set. Many teachers would prefer to reverse the order and allow these features to emerge gradually from regional studies before any attempt is made to systematise them. Whichever approach is adopted there is much to be said for selecting at first regions containing elements which have already become familiar by direct experience on the ground. The North East of England, South Wales, industrial Yorkshire and Lancashire and Central Scotland hold many features in common in the pattern, both past and present, of their industrial and urban growth; agricultural changes which affect East Anglia in terms of mechanisation, the use of fertilizers, specialisation and adjustment to markets, apply to most of agricultural Britain; development and conservation in the Scottish Highlands, the Lake District, North and Central Wales and the Pennines all involve questions of afforestation, marginal farming, the use of water resources, recreation and communications in difficult terrain; the large conurbations that stretch from London through the Midlands to Merseyside, and are scattered discontinuously through the rest of industrial Britain, have such common problems as commuting and competition for land among industry, commerce, roads, housing and other social requirements. What is suggested here is that geography teachers should be as much concerned in their regional studies with the similarities between one area and another as with the uniqueness of each area. For it is the similarities that reveal general tendencies and pattern, without which school geography is thrown back to a great deal of memorisation. At this point it is worth recording that more and more schools do not depend solely on the home region for direct experience as a base from which to expand outwards. The practice of visiting places at some distance from the home area is widespread. Many Local Education Authorities maintain residential centres which afford opportunities for extended study of a new environment, and many encourage the use of Field Study Centres, Youth Hostels, Naturalist Centres, Holiday Fellowship Centres and other institutions. If a residential centre is to be exploited to the full the geography teacher should have a clear plan, based upon knowledge of the area to be visited, about the purpose of each field exercise which is undertaken. The awakening of fresh interests, the techniques of study and recording, the choice of subjects whether in the realm of physical or human geography, should all be considered not only as valuable in themselves but as having a wider context, namely the establishment of skills, relationships and ideas which can be applied to understanding other areas.

By way of contrast the teacher may decide to consider the geography of Britain in a unified way, though this may be thought by many teachers to be more suitable for older than younger pupils. A single theme of widespread application arising from the study of data such as may be found in maps or statistics, chosen with a view to demonstrating broad distributions of phenomena such as population densities and land-use, or changes that have taken place in Britain over a period of years, may also be employed as a means of focusing attention on the similarities and differences that exist between areas. The fuel and power industry in Britain is a good example since statistics are readily available from public and commercial authorities, and books[2] and numerous articles[3] are easily accessible. The following figures of coal production tell a plain tale.

	1938	1958	1967/8
Coal production in millions of tons	227	206	171

Not only do they reveal an important change which is taking place in Britain as a whole but they pose the question 'What is happening in the coalfields as mining declines?' A study of the changing economic basis of a group of coalfields may be undertaken to answer

[2] eg Simpson, *Coal and Power Industries in Post War Britain.* Longmans 1966.
[3] eg Various volumes of *Geography* (Geographical Association).

this question. Following from the study of the coal industry the rise of the petroleum industry may be dealt with in its national and regional setting. Petroleum imports have risen from about 12 million tons in 1938 to over 70 million tons in 1969. The refinery industry, which produced about $2\frac{1}{2}$ million tons of petroleum products in 1938 produced over 72 million tons in 1967. The dependence of this industry upon imported raw materials leads to a consideration of the coastal locations of the great refineries and the petro-chemical industry and the growing importance of deep-water facilities for berthing large modern tankers. It also links Britain with its overseas suppliers and demonstrates the involvement of Britain with the Middle East. The C.E.G.B. Statistical Year Book[4] gives information about the electricity industry, which meets a demand that rises by about 7 per cent per year, and which is transforming not only the landscape but also the way of life in homes, industry and transport. The location of generating stations—thermal, nuclear and hydro-electric—can form a useful introduction to regional studies. Similarly the changing agriculture of Britain (handily recorded in the Journals of the Association of Agriculture), maps showing the distribution of population changes or the development of the motorway system, and the location of the motor-vehicle industry, can help pupils to look at general aspects of their country and at the same time lead them to enquire into specific small areas.

In constructing a scheme of work which deals with the geography of the world outside Britain the teacher should be guided on the one hand by affairs which are likely to be matters of public concern for many years to come, and on the other by events which, though comparatively short-lived, stimulate widespread public interest and receive extensive coverage on television and radio and in the press. Teachers have always been aware of the value of current events as vehicles for teaching; volcanic eruptions, catastrophic storms, political events, Royal visits abroad and even Test Matches have been used as means of awakening interest in physical and regional geography. Many events of this kind burst upon the world scene, enjoy a brief blaze of publicity and quickly sink into the limbo of yesterday's news. It is difficult for the teacher to anticipate them in his plan of work. But this is not true of those long-term issues referred to above. These may well afford guidance in the matter of choosing topics and areas for study which may be built into a scheme of work. Some examples are given here but many others will occur to teachers.

---

[4] From the Central Electricity Generating Board, Sudbury House, Newgate St., London, EC1.

1 There are still areas of the world where the lives of communities are closely adjusted to the rhythm of the seasons, the soil, natural vegetation or the wild life or domesticated flocks that yield meat, wool and skins. Central Borneo, the Amazon forests, the Tundra regions and the great arid tracts of the earth all spring to mind as areas where economic life exists at a relatively simple level and strongly influences social customs. Not only do they demonstrate the skill with which people often manage a hostile environment, but they also raise questions which are important for the future of mankind— questions about the nature of the environments themselves and ways in which their resources may be best exploited. In the study of such areas it is well to remember that they are seldom static. Oil is bringing new wealth to the deserts of the Sahara and Arabia and to the wastes of Alaska; the Eskimo plays a part in the early warning system of northern Canada; in parts of Sarawak[5] the shifting agriculture and longhouses are being replaced by settled plantations and villages; in Nigeria there are government sponsored model farming communities which use new agricultural methods; the irrigated lands of Turkestan were, within living memory, occupied by nomadic herdsmen.

2 At the other extreme are the highly developed regions of the world where industry flourishes, where towns and cities abound and are linked with dense networks of communications, where large numbers of people are employed in trade, commerce, education, welfare services and recreations, and where highly productive farming, backed by science, technology and economics, absorbs only a small proportion of the labour force. Britain itself constitutes an example with which selected countries may be compared and contrasted.

3 Between these extremes lies a large range of regions and countries some already well on the way to achieving a high standard of living and others struggling to establish the beginnings of modernised agriculture and industry and adequate social services. The 'developing countries' are especially worthy of study, not only because they focus attention on problems of development and on the various programmes of aid to which wealthier nations are committed, as well as their international political interests, but also because they contain within themselves explosive qualities that cannot be ignored. Rapid changes in the way of life of a people create internal tensions. Moreover large-scale development of resources, or great industrial schemes, are inevitably piece-meal, bringing prosperity to some and not to others. The contrasts between northern Venezuela and the

---

[5] H. Hulig *Transactions of the Institute of British Geographers* No. 47. Sept 1969.

Orinoco basin, between the coastal fringe of Brazil and the vast interior, between the oil towns of Libya and the impoverished deserts, between industrial India and the farming areas are all potential sources of friction. Boys and girls who have never examined the problems of developing countries are ill-fitted to take an intelligent interest in world affairs as they grow older.

The three broad categories mentioned above may well form a framework which would assist the teacher in his selection of regions or countries to be studied. There are, too, general topics which will continue to exercise the thoughts of men and shape the destinies of countries. The power sources of the world—now heavily weighted in favour of oil; the discovery and exploitation of metalliferous ores, notably those of iron, copper, aluminium, tin and those used in alloys; food supplies and industrial crops; the exploitation and management of forest resources; all of these involve some consideration of standards of living, conservation, trade, and politics. Racial differences, present in a relatively minor sense in Britain, but matters of great concern in USA, Malaya and parts of Africa, are often linked with economic, social and political differences. The tropical world has its special problems of disease and soil management.[6]

Over-population—a relative term—may be studied in terms of natural resources, degrees of exploitation and trade. Conservation has already been mentioned but the special problems of soil and water conservation are becoming urgent in many areas. The pollution of the environment is increasingly claiming the attention of scientists, industrialists and governments, particularly in countries which are highly urbanised and industrialised. Political and economic geography are closely bound up with associations such as the Commonwealth, Comecon, the European Economic Community, and the Pan-African movement.

The geography teacher has an important part to play in helping boys and girls to understand issues such as those outlined above. In selecting the examples which he chooses from regional studies or general topics, he must be guided, to some extent, by the resources at his command. His purpose will be achieved if he places each example in its national or world setting after it has been studied in some detail. In some cases it may be possible for groups of pupils to study different examples. But the dangers of isolated studies can be averted only if the teacher consciously helps his pupils to recognise that the case studies are representative of widespread phenomena, which may be identified and located on the globe.

[6] Pierre Gourou *The Tropical World.* Longmans 1954.

D

Before leaving the question of selection two other questions may be asked. First, what is the place of descriptive regional geography? Second, what is the place of physical geography? The first is easier to answer than the second. Almost any of the topics or regions dealt with above involve an element of description. Films, descriptive accounts in books, oral accounts by the teacher, an examination of various kinds of data and information, all partake of the nature of description. But description is not, except for the least able pupils, an end in itself. Description of a selected group of areas can be part of the process of feeding in material which is to be analysed; it is harnessed to the end in view, which may be an attempt to educe basic concepts (such as the prevalence of disease and leached soils in many tropical areas), or an attempt to focus attention on a widespread problem (such as soil erosion). Description may, on the other hand, be an appropriate end in itself when it is achieved by the pupils after studying a variety of data; in such a case it calls for the use of information in order to arrive at a balanced picture of the topic or area under consideration. In its more refined form this is an exacting intellectual process, more suited to the mature and thoughtful pupil than to the immature, but limited forms of description may be achieved at a simple level by pupils at all ages. Descriptive geography may thus be seen in two distinct roles, as a means or an end, both requiring the exercise of reasoning on the part of the pupils. Without the process of reasoning, inductive or deductive, description becomes little more than an exercise in memorisation. But every teacher is sensitive to those occasions when pupils are deeply moved by splendour, beauty, and awe in the works of nature and man, and there are times when description must be left to do its own work. Geography is concerned with the affective domain as well as the cognitive domain.[7]

Of physical geography it must be said at the outset that pupils destined for continued academic education beyond school would be poorly served if it were neglected. For them an orderly treatment of the physical basis of land-forms, climate and bio-geography can provide both a stimulating intellectual experience and an appreciation of the complex natural framework within which human activities are conducted. Much time and effort can, however, be wasted by introducing a comprehensive and logical approach to physical geography early in the secondary school course. For younger pupils it is sufficient to deal with specific questions concerning land-forms and climate as they arise and in the simplest way which is appropriate to the task in hand. A grasp of the patterns of climate distribution

---

[7] Bloom and Kratwohl *A Taxonomy of Educational Objectives* Books I and II.

is far more important than an analysis of geomorphological phenomena, and even then any attempt at detailed explanations of cause
and process is unprofitable. At a time when geography is unlikely
to receive a greater share of the school day it behoves the teacher
to use time in ways which are most profitable to the pupils. For
the great majority there can be little profit in a thorough study of
the various types of volcanic rocks, extrusive and intrusive, of
desert morphology, of drainage patterns, of glacial phenomena,
of high and low pressure systems in relation to continental and
oceanic climates, of an explanation and classification of rainfall
causes and of many other topics dealt with in text-books of physical
geography. Significant effects, rather than causes and processes, are
more likely to be of value. This is not to suggest that physical
geography should disappear from courses of work for all but older
pupils. It has been stated earlier that the home region and areas
which pupils may visit for a short period of residence provide
opportunities of studying the real world, and it is here that the
teacher may stimulate an interest in physical geography. If a school
has access to a coast processes of erosion and deposition, tides and
currents and the gradation of beach materials may be observed,
measured, classified and recorded in a scientific way. Some schools
may be well placed for the study of streams and rivers, slopes and
surface run-off; others may be near to a succession of rock outcrops
which is reflected in surface features; some inhabit an area with
strongly marked glacial features; many are able to undertake a
serious study of soils; and all have access to weather which, in a
progressive course, can lead to an understanding of the popular
weather map and the effects of the main air-masses which affect our
climate. Physical geography based on direct experience cannot
provide a comprehensive course, but if it consists of active exploration supported by suitable techniques of examination and recording
it is more likely to create an interest in, and an awareness of, the
physical world than the highly generalised accounts and diagrams
which abound in text-books. Pupils trained in the study of real
phenomena have a sure foundation upon which a more systematic
treatment may be built at a later stage.

The question of selection has been dealt with in some detail since it
lies at the heart of syllabus-making. Other elements introduced
earlier in this chapter are treated briefly at this stage either because
they have already been touched upon in this section or because they
are elaborated on in subsequent chapters.

Skills and the Use of Evidence
It is one thing to pass information on to pupils and expect them to

remember it, and quite a different thing to train them to use sources of information in order to reach conclusions. As a method of teaching the former covers ground more quickly but it may leave the pupil without independence of thought or judgment. The latter is a slower process but it helps the pupil to stand on his own feet. The busy teacher may find it necessary to employ both methods but there is a growing tendency to teach pupils how to learn. It is a commonplace claim for geography as a school subject that it trains pupils in the use of maps of all kinds. Maps, however, are not the only kinds of evidence that geographers use. Pupils can learn to collect and evaluate evidence of many kinds in the field and time spent by the teacher in teaching field-work techniques is rewarded by the growth of self-assurance in pupils. Similarly pupils can learn to use pictures, graphs, statistics and written accounts, to name a few of the sources upon which description or conclusions may be based. The teacher's part in this process demands the utmost skill. Not only must he judge the difficulty of the evidence which pupils may successfully handle but he must also define the purposes for which the evidence is being examined. The questions to which answers are sought may be simple or complex. 'The passage of a warm front over East Anglia during the morning is forecast; take hourly readings and record the changes that take place in temperature, rainfall, clouds and wind direction'. This is a straightforward task involving simple skills and flexibility in organisation; but to interpret the records and compare them with the weather map is more difficult. Or again pupils in a farming area might be asked to compare life in their own area with that in an Indian village, the evidence being a knowledge of the home area and a film and a written account of an Indian village. As a simple exercise the comparison might be concerned with homes, clothing, food, dress and the farming year. Taken further it might involve a consideration of differences in climate and population densities. At a higher level questions of education, religion, new farming methods and Government development plans could be introduced; and statistics showing the proportions of the working population engaged in agriculture in selected countries in Europe, North and South America, and Asia might be examined. Geography taught in this way provides not only knowledge but tools of learning which can be sharpened by discussion and used in future life.

General Concepts
Geography teachers have long been accustomed to introducing their pupils to general relationships that exist between phenomena, and it has become increasingly common to use a particular example in one situation as a means of discovering these relationships before applying them to other situations. This is done much more commonly

in physical geography than human, and in human geography it has been applied more to rural than urban studies. For example the effects of cold and warm ocean currents on the climate of neighbouring land masses, rainshadow, the distribution of natural forests and grassland, the influence of climates and soils on the broad distributions of crops, the changing characteristics of a river valley from its source to mouth, and the association of mineral deposits with geological formations, have regularly been taught as general concepts which can be widely applied in describing and explaining locations and areal differentiations. It has been less common for teachers to concern themselves with general ideas about settlement patterns, central places, urban functions and morphology, the effects of markets on farming practice, and many other topics in the realm of economic and social geography and transport. Yet it is general concepts in these fields that are most likely to be of value in bringing to pupils an understanding of their own country and of other countries with a complex and highly developed economic structure. Quantitative methods, statistics and models which can be tested against reality, which are beginning to find a place in schools, afford means of dealing with many kinds of information in ways which permit spatial and other relationships to be educed and stated with varying degrees of precision. General concepts which can be brought to light by such means represent economies of thought which are particularly valuable in disentangling the many threads that are woven into the complicated fabric of modern society.

Applying Geography
Enough has already been stated in this chapter to indicate that school geography is no longer confined to detached study of the distribution of natural features and human activities on the face of the earth. If it is designed to help boys and girls to understand their environment it is also concerned with dynamic forces that are re-shaping the environment, with problems of change, with economic, political and social questions. There are many occasions when geographers may find it necessary to join forces with teachers of history, economics, science and mathematics; and perhaps some when co-operation with teachers of modern languages, art, music and religion may be fruitful. Expeditions in difficult country may invite joint planning and execution by teachers of geography and physical education. Geography too has its links with literature. There are few schools that have sufficient flexibility in their organisation to encourage frequent enterprises involving teachers from two or more departments, but there are many examples of team work, sometimes on a temporary and sometimes on a more permanent basis. This is to be encouraged when a wide-ranging topic is being studied, for though

the geography teacher is well equipped to handle matters over a wide field of enquiry, he, more than anyone else, realises the enrichment that comes from consultation with those who profess other disciplines.

Sometimes the geography department may have to work in isolation from others. Even then it may, on occasion, approach its tasks by a fresh route. For example the geography of USA and the USSR could be dealt with by a traditional treatment of general and regional studies in each country, or it could take the form of an attempt to examine the question 'what are the relative strengths and weaknesses of these two great world powers?' The second approach might start with a general comparison of man-power, natural resources, food production, industrial development, climates, communications (including access to the oceans), and degrees of economic self-sufficiency. A study of maps of population distribution, of the disposition of industrial plant and of road and rail networks might be undertaken in the context of vulnerability to attack. The attitudes of neighbouring countries might be discussed. Such a study, carried out in some detail, would eventually cover much the same ground as a traditional study, but it would have the advantage of possessing a purpose of real significance to older boys and girls. In a legitimate sense this can be called 'applied geography' since the geographer is bringing his knowledge and skills to bear on a problem. Needless to say, the combined efforts of economist, historian and geographer could bring greater authenticity to a project of this nature.

A number of issues raised in this chapter are expanded in later chapters, but before embarking on them some thought must be given to geography teaching in Comprehensive Schools.

Comprehensive Schools
The following sections are concerned with a few problems which are specific to Comprehensive Schools rather than with syllabuses and teaching methods. They arise from organisational matters and current opinions about social grouping.

Group Work
For the first two or three years of the course (assuming that pupils begin at eleven years of age) the geography teacher may have to manage groups which comprise a wide spread of ability. In such circumstances the class lesson in which all pupils carry out the same work cannot do justice to the differing requirements and potentials of the pupils, and some form of sub-division into groups will be necessary. To many teachers in Secondary schools this will be a departure from established practice. An example has been given

earlier of lessons, one on clothing and another on Japan, in which tasks were organised to suit the different stages of development that groups of pupils had reached, without destroying the common theme shared by the whole class. Many topics in geography lend themselves to this sort of sub-division into elements with differing degrees of complexity. An example follows in which the study of rivers is analysed into components of varying difficulty set out in stages; the example is, in no sense, exhaustive, nor have the stages been experimentally tested (Table 1). The matrix does not include the early work of the primary school but it does include work normally done in Sixth Forms at stage 5.

Table 1

Stages	Sources and destination of water	Physical features	Human Geography
1	Rainfall: surface run-off; springs; flow to lakes and seas.	Current; load; erosion of banks; floods.	Fish supplies; irrigation.
2	Glaciers and snow-melt—seasonal variations in flow. The water-cycle.	Valley forms—upper, middle and lower courses. Waterfalls.	Water supply and early village sites. River-mouth ports; tidal estuaries and docks; water power for mills and early factories.
3	Inland drainage and salt lakes. Seepage; water-table. Artesian wells.	Watersheds; catchment areas; open estuaries and deltas.	Transport (eg Rhine and Danube). Bridges and bridging points. Hydro-electric power.
4	Evaporation losses (Nile, Indus) Swallow-holes.	Gorges, meanders, deposition, levees, ox-bow lakes; flood plains.	Industrial needs for water; effluent and pollution. Siting of thermal electric power stations.
5	Association of river regimes and climatic regimes. Fossil water in arid zones.	Drainage patterns. Rejuvenation; incised meanders, river-capture; wind-gaps; misfit streams. Analytical work on stream flow, meanders, pool and riffle sequences.	Modern water supply. Problems of conflicting demands (a) for water (b) for land use in catchment areas.

In a mixed-ability class different groups would be working on different parts of the matrix according to their capacity and previous experience. Boys and girls who quickly grasp the arguments, relationships and concepts involved at each stage would move on to the next;

some might need to work out several exercises or study several examples of a component before moving on. Only a few examples have been included in the matrix; many others will occur to the teacher.

A large number of general topics in geography can be set out in this way. For example forests can be dealt with under headings such as types of trees, climatic associations, distributions of main types of forest, exploitation of forested areas and problems of development; settlement may be studied in terms of sizes of units, functions, urban morphology and distributions. In some cases the components may be studied in the field, in others books and displays of materials may be consulted, exercises may be worked out, or role-playing games may be employed; it goes without saying that many components may be dealt with through the medium of exposition by the teacher or discussion with him. Regional geography, as has already been demonstrated, can be studied by resolving the area or country under consideration into components of varying complexity. A study of Brazil could be introduced by the teacher drawing attention to some salient features such as its great extent, the broad physical divisions and the great areas of forest and natural grassland. Thereafter pupils might work at different levels. Some might be concerned with descriptive accounts of Brasilia, the Amazon river, equatorial forests, and a coffee plantation; others might draw climatic graphs of stations in the major vegetation zones and compare them with similarly placed stations in Africa; others might attempt to answer the question 'Why is the bulk of the population to be found within a few hundred miles of the coast?'; others might prepare an account of mining and manufacturing in Brazil.

Group work of this kind requires good departmental organisation and generous resources for learning. Much of the study will be based on atlases and textbooks; some of it will depend for intimate detail on articles in newspapers and their supplements, or picture-rich publications like the Geographical Magazine; some will use well known reference sources; some will be based on information sheets and work sheets prepared by the staff for use in a number of Forms and possibly over several years. Information sheets for Commonwealth Studies have been produced for many years by the Commonwealth Institute and a good many schools make use of them. They provide a model for teachers unaccustomed to them; frequently very simple versions may be produced by the school to suit the capacities of the slow learners, for their basic skills, however humble, should be put to use whenever possible.

Inter-departmental arrangements
Under this somewhat clumsy sub-title are included two organisational devices affecting geography, both of which have been introduced into schools in recent years. They have one common feature, namely, that geography appears on the time-table in association with one or more other subjects. In one case it may be part of some form of integrated studies and in the other it may be an attempt to offer departmental heads greater flexibility in the management of time.

(a) *Integrated studies*
Something has already been said about integrated studies. The importance of the teacher's role in recording and controlling the geographical content, which has already been referred to, takes on greater significance as pupils grow older. Some will be preparing for external examinations; those who are not should be given the opportunity of applying their geographical skills and knowledge to the study of useful and relevant topics. In both cases a foundation of geography is required and this will not be laid by the haphazard pursuit of one enquiry after another. The teacher must therefore be active in manipulating both the choice of topics and the way in which they are developed to ensure that objectives somewhat in advance of those set out for the Middle School are kept to the forefront, though quite clearly, some modifications must be made to suit the slower learners and the very able. A course in the third year which concentrates on the study of important issues at home and abroad should afford a satisfying experience for pupils who will soon drop geography and, at the same time, continue to expand the skills and understanding of the rest.

(b) *Time allocations*
Blocked time arrangements[8] offer a chance of re-apportioning time among several departments. For example a block of six weekly periods might be available to the history, geography and religious education departments. The block might consist of two afternoons each of three periods, or a morning of four periods and a second block of two periods. Provided they can share time equitably over a term or an even longer period the departmental heads gain a great deal in flexibility. For example simultaneous block time-tabling across a 'band' of three Forms would permit the geographer to claim the whole six periods with one Form for the first month while his colleagues made similar claims for the other two Forms. At the

[8] See *Trends in Education* April 1970 'The Balance of the Curriculum in Secondary Schools'.

end of a month the Forms would change their subject. In the course of a term each Form would have received its due allocation of time, but in a substantial block. Such an arrangement would permit field work to be done in school time, or general topics and regional studies to be dealt with intensively. The example quoted is but one of a number of possible ways of managing time allocations. Geography has much to gain from such arrangements for its purposes are frequently frustrated by the two or three single teaching periods which it normally receives in a week. Moreover, if the resources of the neighbourhood and the geography room are used fully to bring variety into the work the range of activities which is possible makes it unlikely that the work will generate boredom or lose pace. Nothing that has been stated in this paragraph should be interpreted as advocating any particular form of reallocating time. The fact is that the way in which time is used in the secondary school is being questioned and there are schools which are experimenting with novel time-table arrangements. The geography teacher should be prepared to promote and exploit developments which give him a more favourable setting for the pursuit of his objectives.

Geography rooms
Planning for future developments must always be based upon past experience and assumptions about the future. Bearing in mind that some margin of doubt must always exist it is possible to make estimates of the need for geography rooms in future schools. If it can be assumed that the overall place of geographical studies in the curriculum will not change substantially, an average 8-form entry school would need three or four rooms equipped for teaching geography.

It is tempting to claim a suite of rooms in a closely tied geography department, but if all subjects made the same claim the school would be inexorably divided into self-enclosed subject departments with little encouragement for inter-disciplinary work. Geography would be well served if it were provided with a well-equipped main centre for the subject and if other rooms were conveniently placed for co-operative ventures with other subjects. For example one subsidiary geography room might be associated with a humanities group of rooms including history and economics, and another with an environmental studies group including general science and rural studies. In each case the geography base would need a good supply of maps and visual aids but it could share a work-space and some equipment with its neighbours.

Of the main geography centre it might be asked, how can the available space be best disposed to serve the needs of pupils and teachers? It has long been claimed that a geography room should be 960 square feet or more in area. This claim is based on another—that geography is a practical subject which needs a good deal of space. There are occasions when geography needs all the space that such a room affords. But surveys[9] show that, even when space is available, for a very high proportion of geography lessons the pupils are seated at desks or tables using maps, atlases, books and other reference materials, or sharing in class lessons with or without visual aids; in such lessons the free working space is not used by the class and, not uncommonly, a group of Sixth-formers may be working there. The great majority of geography lessons could be carried out in a somewhat smaller room provided that there was access to an adjoining practical work space for those occasions when models are in use or being made, large runs of maps set up, extensive displays being mounted, or when pupils are working in dispersed groups. There is a need for teachers to consider different arrangements of geography teaching spaces in order that the best compromise may be achieved to satisfy the many and varied demands that may be made upon them.

[9] Carried out by HM Inspectors.

5

The Methods of the Geographer in the Field

Interest in fieldwork has grown rapidly in recent years, partly as a result of the requirements of certain CSE and GCE Examining Boards, but mainly because teachers have shown a growing appreciation of its value. Training in its methods has become a prominent element in University and College courses. The place of fieldwork in the curriculum varies greatly from school to school. Some teachers regard it as an essential part of each year's programme from the First form to the Sixth. Some pursue a less ambitious scheme by introducing fieldwork in alternate years; and some do little or none at all. When fieldwork is omitted or relegated to a minor role there are often serious difficulties. There may be internal obstacles in the school—staffing problems, unsympathetic colleagues or, more commonly, an inviolable timetable which imprisons the whole of the school's activities. Sometimes teachers lack confidence in planning fieldwork and carrying out exercises which are suitable for their pupils, but in the last few years so many books have been published and so many courses run on fieldwork techniques that this is no longer common. Local Education Authorities vary in their attitudes towards and their support for fieldwork. Some take the view that they are justified in spending public funds on outdoor work only when it is specified by an Examining Board as an essential part of the syllabus. Some schools have found it difficult to obtain finance for short journeys, particularly when part or the whole of the cost falls on the pupils. There is, however, evidence that all these difficulties are diminishing, and that the value of fieldwork as an integral part of school geography now receives general recognition.

It is, of course, reasonable to ask that teachers should be aware of the need for economy in preparing fieldwork programmes, and it is to be expected that a Local Education Authority should look with an inauspicious eye on plans to conduct expensive excursions to distant places when the resources of the school's immediate vicinity remain unused. The local environment as a field laboratory possesses special advantages. For both younger and older pupils the home

48

region is the only one where continuous study to observe change may be carried out by repeated visits over a period of days, weeks or even years. With the home region the pupils' lives are intimately associated, and an understanding of the forces that have shaped it in the past and are reshaping it for the future has an immediate relevance for older boys and girls. Many techniques of observation and measurement, the use of instruments of many kinds and methods of recording can all be learned inexpensively in the school's neighbourhood. If boys and girls are well trained on their home ground then time can be used to greater advantage when a visit is made to a distant area. It is always regrettable when the precious time afforded by a short period of residence in an exciting new area is frittered away in teaching simple techniques such as walking on a compass bearing, following a route on a map, or using a clinometer or a maximum and minimum thermometer, all of which could have been dealt with at home. While the home region may provide extensive opportunities for progressive field studies the value of a period of residence in a contrasting area has been increasingly recognised by teachers and Education Authorities. The Field Studies Council now has nine centres, and about forty per cent of the students attend for geographical studies, the majority coming from Sixth forms. Over sixty Local Education Authorities maintain residential centres at which fieldwork may be carried out; many others give generous financial support and encouragement for fieldwork based on Field Study Centres, Youth Hostels, Naturalist Centres, Holiday Fellowship Hostels and other institutions. There are, too, organisations such as the Brathay Trust, the Yorkshire School Exploration Society and the Boys' and Girls' Schools' Exploration societies, which undertake field studies abroad. A few schools and colleges have acquired their own residential centres, and many teachers make private arrangements for carrying out fieldwork away from the home area. Some schools have acquired camping equipment which affords a temporary base for fieldwork.

An analysis of selected writings by a good many authors of books and articles on fieldwork shows the importance that is placed upon observation, making records, seeking explanations, developing a 'seeing eye', and devising an active role for pupils in the field. In more recent works measurement, analysis and the search for correlations begin to appear, and more rarely the linking of fieldwork with hypotheses. There are, it is clear, different kinds of fieldwork and this chapter is concerned with an examination of their various styles and purposes. Reference has already been made to the importance of field experience in primary schools, in which the aims are largely the establishment of vocabulary which is both enlarged and rendered more discriminating by discussion, the awakening of interest in the many components that make a total environment, the opportunities for children to explore features which interest them, and the stimulation for making records of many kinds. Every one of these simply stated aims is relevant to fieldwork at all levels, but when pupils have reached the stage where they can seek explanations and relationships fieldwork takes on other dimensions.

At the outset the distinction must be drawn between field teaching and fieldwork. In the former it is the teacher who examines, describes and explains the features selected for study; he may demonstrate methods of carrying out fieldwork and recording, he may answer questions or stimulate discussion, and he usually requires the pupils to make records of his teaching. In fieldwork it is the pupils who take over the active role of examining, describing and explaining. The difference between the two is usually revealed in the pupils' workbooks. Good fieldwork is usually based on good field teaching. There are occasions when the teacher finds it necessary to do a great deal of teaching, particularly when the pupils have had no previous experience of the elements with which the exercise is concerned. There are other occasions when the work may be placed wholly in the hands of the pupils, who often work best in small groups. More commonly teaching and fieldwork are intermingled. One of the most satisfying experiences for the geography teacher is the successful accomplishment of fieldwork exercises by pupils who, under his guidance, have mastered the skills of observation, measurement and recording which give them an interest in questions posed by the environment and confidence in their ability to seek answers. If field teaching does not emancipate pupils to some extent from their dependence on the teacher it will have failed to achieve one of its most important objectives.

Both field teaching and fieldwork require preparation by the teacher. This is best done on the ground, where different kinds of exercises may be chosen to match the stage of development of the pupils. If the work is to be carried out in the vicinity of the school this usually raises few problems since the neighbourhood is usually well known to the teacher. When fieldwork is to be carried out at a distance from the school a preparatory visit, though desirable, may not always be possible. An experienced geographer can learn a great deal from the careful study of maps and publications such as the 'British Landscape Through Maps' series[1] and the many books on local studies which

---

[1] Published by the Geographical Association.

are now available. The difference between the positive and purposeful work that results from thorough preparation, and the tentative approach of the ill-prepared exercise is all too apparent. In preparing for fieldwork faith is a poor substitute for work.

Fieldwork for schools falls into three main categories—descriptive and explanatory, problem-solving and hypothesis-testing. The first category has been widely practised for many years, but the introduction of quantitative methods has promoted an increasing use of enumeration, measurement and sampling; and the greater interest shown by geographers in urban studies is reflected in the schools as teachers have appreciated the range and usefulness of studies which are possible in towns. Reference has been made in earlier chapters to the ways in which a foundation of competence for young children may be laid in outdoor studies. There is little place in fieldwork for the hurried dash across country in a train or coach with a route-map and directions to record isolated pieces of information at selected points. Good fieldwork training is based on a close examination of limited phenomena circumscribed by well defined tasks. The tasks may be suggested by the teacher or by the pupils; sometimes the pupils will devise their own techniques for carrying out the work, but more frequently the teacher will need to demonstrate how to go about the work, especially if the use of instruments is involved, or if recording is to be done in an unfamiliar way. The decision whether the teacher shall direct the work in the field itself or whether he can offer adequate guidance by means of questionnaires or instruction sheets depends on the nature of the exercise and the previous experience of the pupils. When a class occupies a safe vantage point such as a hill or a flat-topped building, a great deal of work can be done with a large group; practice in field-sketching can often be best supervised when the class is assembled together. There are, however, problems associated with teaching a large group out of doors, not the least of which is oral communication against a background of competing noise. When the class can safely be left to pursue investigations in small groups with work-sheets the teacher is free to move among them giving help where it is most needed and giving instruction in special techniques such as the use of the compass or clinometer or ways of recording traffic flows. It is only when pupils have had experience of studying limited parts of an environment that they can be expected to undertake the more exacting work of attempting a description of a small region and an explanation of the relationships that can be discerned among various elements in it.

Work sheets for fieldwork can be adjusted to the stage of development of the pupils. The following examples are taken from schools and field study centres. They reveal great variety in the kinds of guidance that teachers find necessary, and variation in attitude to degrees of precision:

1 **Sand dunes**

   (a) Location of survey......... (b) Date......... (c) Time...............
   What is the direction of alignment of the dunes?
   Does this tell you anything about prevailing winds?
   How high do you estimate the biggest ones?
   Draw a cross section of a dune to show its shape and height, and plot the vegetation growing on the outer and inner sides of the dune.
   Name three shrubs found on the dunes, and three plants peculiar to dunes.

2 **River study**

   From the mouth of the River Kenfig (GR 780834) trace the course of the river half a mile inland and record the following:

   Extent of high tide penetration. What is the evidence for this?
   Width and depth of river (at its centre) at intervals of 100 yards.
   The dominant plants on the banks to a depth of 20 yards from the river.
   Whether the river is slow-moving or fast-moving.
   Evidence of silting or erosion.
   Evidence of a salt marsh. Map its area and identify the main flora.
   Signs of animal life bordering the river.
   Draw a map to illustrate the discoveries you have made and diagrams on any specific topics which interest you.

3 **Cultivation on concave slopes**

   (NB: arrangements had already been made with farmers to visit fields and each group of pupils was allocated to a farm.)
   On the farm maps mark arable land (A) and grassland (G).
   Measure the angles of slope of the steepest arable fields and those with the lowest slopes.
   Take soil samples from the lowest arable field and the highest arable field.
   What are the depths of the A horizons?
   What use is made of the fields immediately above the steepest arable field?
   Take a soil sample from the field above the steepest arable field, and about 50 yards above it. What is the depth of the A horizon?
   What is the slope at this point?
   Mark on your map the positions of your soil samples.

In this exercise nine farms were visited; the classroom analysis of the results was concerned with using regression techniques to examine relations between

(a) slope and pH coefficient

(b) slope and depth of A horizon of soils

(c) maximum slope ploughed in each farm.

4   Shopping facilities in a New Town

Count the number of shops of the following kinds which are to be found at the neighbourhood centres at Bennettsgate, Queens Square, Long Chaulden, and in Hemel Hempstead Town Centre.

Food shops: General stores
                      Grocers
                      Bakers and Confectioners
                      Greengrocers
                      Butchers
                      Fresh fish and fried fish

Supermarkets
Chemists
Children's clothing
Clothing (women)
Clothing (men)
Shoes
{ Sweets and tobacco
{ Newsagent
Ladies' Hairdresser
Men's hairdresser
Dry Cleaner
Launderette
Public houses
Cafés and Restaurants
Hardware, paint, wallpaper, garden equipment
Electrical goods and gramophone records
Furniture
Jeweller and fancy goods
Books and Stationery
Departmental stores (include Woolworths, Marks and Spencers).

Account for the differences between the neighbourhood centres and the Town centre. What shops would you expect to find in the neighbourhood centres which were not visited? Check your answer by visiting them.

5 **Housing**
On the 25-inch map of Sunderland mark out two rectangles 20,000 square yards in area (they need not necessarily be the same shape) to cover housing areas at Redby and the Red House estate. Count the number of houses in each rectangle and calculate the housing densities.
Visit each area and make notes of the main building materials used for walls and roofs; sketch the common types of windows and doors in each area.
From the rating office find the dates of building of ten houses distributed over each rectangle at Redby and the Red House.
What changes have taken place in housing since the houses at Redby were built?

Each of these exercises is concerned with description and explanation and the fourth exercise contains an element of 'prediction'. They may be compared with the two of a group of Sixth form exercises carried out by an Oxfordshire school in Devon, which are problem-solving exercises.

1 There is a proposal to build a boating lake in the area below the sea wall at GR 431293. If the scheme is carried out it may well affect the movement of pebbles along the storm beach. Before construction it is necessary to study the movement of pebbles in the area under varying wind and beach conditions. In what direction are the pebbles moving? At what speed? What is the weight of pebbles moved? Which pebbles move most quickly?

2 Last winter part of the 14th Century bridge spanning the River Torridge at Bideford fell down, cutting the town in two and breaking the A 39 trunk road. Temporary repairs have been carried out but the disaster will naturally speed plans for the construction of a new bridge and, at the same time, a road to by-pass the town. Carry out a survey to establish the best situations for the new bridge and by-pass systems.

What was interesting about the reports on these problems was not only the techniques employed by the students but also their critical comments on the limitations of their results. The maps, statistical summaries, graphical work and analyses were carried out with meticulous care, but the students pointed out the need for extending the work over longer periods to obtain more reliable results and recorded their views on improvements which could be made in their own methods of work.

Not all problem-solving exercises need be as sophisticated as those just described. There are many straightforward problems which pupils might find interesting and rewarding, and for which they might devise their own methods of work. Some examples are given here.

1   What difference does the holiday season make to the traffic density and speed of traffic flow? (In the vicinity of a seaside town.) This is an exercise in which a structured sample of traffic counts is necessary. A further development could be an estimate of the main bottlenecks based on a study of maps, followed by a check on the ground.
2   What is the time lag between heavy rainfall and a marked rise in the river level? Does it vary between winter and summer? What period of drought is necessary to reduce the river to a point at which lateral erosion is unlikely? In these circumstances does lateral erosion cease on straight stretches before it does on bends?
3   What difference does a southerly aspect on a slope make to mid-day soil temperatures at a depth of (a) 10 cm and (b) 20 cm as compared with a north-facing slope? Do the differences exist on sunless days as well as on sunny days?
4   When did slate cease to be used as the common roofing material for houses in the town?
5   What changes in farming have taken place in the neighbourhood in the last twenty years in respect of (a) crops, (b) livestock, (c) the use of machinery and fertilizers, and (d) the markets to which produce is sent? How do these local changes compare with national changes in farming?
6   What changes have taken place in the use of electricity in homes during the last forty years? (Enquire from parents and grand-parents about their homes.) What local industries use large amounts of electricity?
7   Why are road-widening operations being carried out on some main roads and not on others?

Other questions might involve the origins of local supplies of water, meat, vegetables and milk. Among the many questions that boys and girls ask about their home area there are some that readily adapt themselves to problem-solving exercises which involve the same kinds of skills and lead to the same kinds of knowledge as descriptive and explanatory studies. They have the added advantages of immediacy and relevance.

The third category of fieldwork—hypothesis-testing—provides a direct link with theoretical geography. Pupils who have made studies of real situations are able to produce models or theories about the ways in which elements are related to one another in space. Some theories are relatively simple in their logic and easy to test. An example is quoted in Chapter 3 in which variations in the depth of top-soil across a valley section were predicted on theoretical grounds; the theoretical variations were tested by examining the ground itself. At the other end of the scale the Sixth form student who has considered Von Thunen's model of land use around a central city may wish to test the hypothesis that the intensity of land use will decrease as distance from the town increases. He will devise a scheme for collecting data by means of transects or structured sampling and seek verification of his hypothesis in the field. Or he may develop a hypothesis that land use is closely related to the underlying geology and carry out field investigations to test it. Examples are quoted by Everson and Fitzergerald[2] of the range of goods and services which can be expected in settlements of various sizes; they provide useful hypothetical models which can easily be tested in the field. The distribution of petrol-stations in relation to main roads, the town centre and housing areas can be theoretically plotted on a map; while precise location is not possible a likely distribution may be achieved which approaches the reality. There is no place in geography for hypotheses which are not well grounded on relevant theory and reality. It is, however, credible that decisions made by the great chain stores, the owners of petrol stations, and farmers are based on factors which are widely accepted as being significant to their purposes. It is the general application of these factors which brings a large measure of order and consistency to human geography. Descriptive fieldwork may not always reveal the bases for decision-making which profoundly influence the rural and urban landscape. One of the main purposes of a hypothetical approach to fieldwork is to help pupils to appreciate certain ways in which the physical world and human purposes conspire to produce recognisable patterns of distribution and behaviour.

[2] *Concepts in Geography* Book I Settlement Patterns. Longmans 1969.

6

The Methods of the Geographer in the Classroom

A good deal has already been written in earlier pages on the methods of the geographer. The purpose of this chapter is to focus attention on a few important principles which underlie changes that have been taking place in teaching the subject in the classroom. The balance between indoor and outdoor work in terms of the amount of time that can be spent on each must always be heavily weighted on the side of the former. But as far as teaching methods are concerned there are close parallels between them. The distinction that has been drawn between field teaching and fieldwork applies to the classroom. Class-teaching or group-teaching, in which the teacher is engaged in exposition, has its counterpart in classwork in which the pupils are pursuing enquiries through the study of books, maps, pictures and other materials. Description and explanation, which dominated school geography for many years, have been joined by problem-solving and hypothesis testing in the classroom as they have in the field. And just as the teacher gradually leads his pupils by way of limited field studies to the more complex inter-relationships of the small region, so he approaches the generalisations encompassed in the study of large areas or wide-ranging topics by means of case-studies. All these changes reflect two dominant trends, the one concerned with the general educational process and the other with the body of geographical knowledge and skills appropriate to pupils in school.

An increasing proportion of the pupils entering the secondary school have been accustomed to working in small groups, pursuing their own interests, using a variety of learning materials and drawing their own conclusions. To them the teacher is a source of encouragement, guidance and support rather than a source of 'knowledge to be acquired and facts to be stored'.[1] In the secondary schools there is evidence[2] that pupils place a high value on more practical work and a greater relevance of subject matter to the modern world. This involvement of pupils as partners in their own education points to the changing pupil-teacher relationship which is to be seen in the classroom. No

---

[1] Hadow Report 1931.
[2] Schools Council Enquiry 1 *Young School Leavers* HMSO 1968.

longer does the teacher find it necessary to occupy the central role for every lesson, using visual aids, wall-maps and oral presentation in class teaching. This is not because class teaching is considered to have lost its value; it still has an important part in the educational process, particularly when new subject matter is broached, a fresh topic is to be introduced, general problems have to be discussed, or an exchange of ideas and opinions is to be stimulated. But teachers are increasingly concerned with helping their pupils to acquire the skills of learning and to undertake the study of topics in which they have a special interest. For this reason many geography departments have built up supplies of questionnaires, work sheets and outline maps associated with themes which have proved successful. These refer the pupils to sources of information relevant to their enquiries. When work is organised in this way the class is dispersed in small groups and the teacher is available for consultation and advice. 'Learning how to learn' is a time-consuming process and the teacher who thus stresses the quality of learning has to be prepared (except in the case of abler pupils) for a diminution in the quantity of traditional geography to which the pupils may be exposed.

Is there, then, an essential body of geographical knowledge which schemes of work should encompass? It is doubtful whether a representative group of geography teachers would agree in detail on an answer to this question. There would probably be strong support for a sound knowledge of the home region and Britain; some would argue for the inclusion of Western Europe, others for the Commonwealth, others for the great World Powers, others for the underdeveloped countries. Few would take the view that a continent-by-continent survey of the world is either practical or relevant to modern needs. Opinions on the extent to which a systematic treatment of physical geography is desirable would differ, but there would probably be many in favour of concepts involving, for example, the natural regions of the world, major distribution patterns and the varying relationships between human activity and environment. The requirements of the Examining Boards, both GCE and CSE have certainly moved in the direction of selectivity. On what principles should selection be based? There is a strong case for basing syllabuses of work on important types of geographical environment, the actual examples being left to the teacher to decide in the light of available resources and the changing panorama of world events. Each type should be studied as a piece of contemporary living geography in its own right, and, whenever pupils are capable of it, as a means of illustrating general concepts.

For the purpose of school geography the types might be chosen from among a number of broad classes.

(a) The 'natural regions' afford an important class which may be studied in relatively simple or more complex terms. 'With reference to the habitat and its significance we have to understand that it is an ecosystem modified by the presence of Man. It is understood that an ecosystem involves areal associates of inter-connected physical and biotic processes such as surface features, climate, water, biota and soils. On this basis generally nine major habitats have been identified on the earth's surface such as Dry Lands; the Tropical Forest Lands; the Tropical Woodlands and Savannas; the Mediterranean Lands; the Mid-Latitude Mixed Forest Lands; the Mid-Latitude Grasslands; the Northern Forest Lands; the Polar Lands; the Mountain Lands. These habitats can be considered the major resource base of man's societies.'[3] Considered as 'resource bases' the natural regions provide the framework within which agricultural activities take place, the nature and degree of exploitation varying from subsistence farming to elementary and advanced commercial agriculture. The types chosen for study should include examples of both the habitats and the varying degrees of intensity with which man uses them, and should take account of changes which are taking place. For examples studies of tropical forest habitats might embody subsistence agriculture in the Amazon Basin and West Africa, the government-sponsored farm settlements of Eastern Nigeria,[4] the intensive farming of Southern India or Java, and plantation agriculture in Malaya; case studies of arid lands would deal with nomadic pastoralism, oasis farming and some great irrigation schemes.

(b) Industrial environments, like agricultural environments, vary in character; at one extreme are relatively simple forms of extraction and manufacturing; at the other are complex systems which call for highly developed technologies and managerial skills. For younger pupils examples of communities engaged in extractive industries—timber in Canada, Sweden and Russia, copper and nitrates in Chile, copper in Zambia, iron ore in Liberia and Western Australia, oil in Texas, Saudi Arabia and Venezuela—lead to a consideration of world trade, power supplies and the importance of transport. Great hydro-electric installations at Kitimat and the Kariba Dam may be studied in the context of the physical conditions

---

[3] P. H. Nash *Ekistecs* Vol. 24 No. 143 December 1967.
[4] See *Economic Geography* Vol. 3 No. 3 July 1967.

which favour the production of water power and its importance to countries like Canada, USA, Norway, Switzerland,
Japan and New Zealand. Older pupils may study more
complex industrial environments in Britain, North America,
the Ruhr, the Ukraine and Japan. Comparisons may be made
between the advanced industrial nations and the emergent
countries.

(c) Population studies[5] provide a link between agricultural and
industrial regions. Areas of dense, medium and sparse population may be chosen with a view to understanding the
restraints imposed by certain kinds of environments—for
example deserts, high mountain areas, the sub-polar regions—
and those environments which have promoted high densities of
population, both rural and industrial. Problems of over-
population in relation to food supplies, and the dependence of
industrial nations on raw materials and world trade are topics
more suitable for older than younger pupils. So too are
analyses of percentages of working population engaged in
primary, secondary and tertiary sectors of industry, which
help pupils to appreciate differences in standards of living
which exist among the nations. Urban studies of services,
housing, transport and communications may be undertaken
by younger pupils but questions of rank size, urban hierarchies,
and the problems of great conurbations come at a later stage.
Migration and its consequences raise questions of moral and
political importance in the modern world. The peopling of the
Americas and Australasia by Europeans, the African slave
migrations to the West Indies and the USA, the Chinese in
south-east Asia, the Russian colonisation of Siberia and
minority groups such as the Australian aborigines are matters
of world importance; the presence of coloured citizens in our
own country should be seen in its world setting as part of a
continuing historical process of large-scale movements of
peoples.

(d) Landscape studies may claim a place in their own right or as
a background to human geography. The high mountain zones
of the Tertiary orogeny, with their rugged peaks and icefields,
the deep gorges of the upper Indus and the Colorado, the vast
plains of the Plate and Mississippi basins, great rivers and
waterfalls, glaciers, volcanoes and the ocean deeps have
always stimulated the imagination and excited the curiosity.
They are as much part of world geography as the lives of

---

[5] See *Population Geography* J. I. Clarke, Pergamon Press 1965.

people. Moreover they profoundly affect human affairs. Whether they occupy a separate place in the scheme of work, or whether they are integrated with human geography is a matter for each teacher to decide, but no course in geography is complete if it fails to convey something of variety and wonder of the earth's physical surface.

This account of some broad categories within which types of environ-may be studied is not intended to be comprehensive. It does, however, provide a framework for selecting topics from which important principles and concepts may be educed. The list may appear unduly large, but if the teacher introduces each theme and then organises work in groups in such a way that each group studies a different example a class may cover a great deal of ground corporately. The comparisons and contrasts that are encompassed in an organised set of studies can form the basis of a discussion during which the teacher focuses attention on the main points. For the first few years of the secondary school course the work should rest firmly on the detailed study of real places rather than generalised accounts. Fortunately the sources of sample studies and case studies are much richer than formerly. Not only are there text-book series which include them but magazines, newspapers, and broadcast series also provide many accounts, frequently with good illustrative material, which can be used. Indeed the choice of examples may sometimes be decided by the resources available.

There is no reason why detailed studies of this kind should exclude the study of countries or large regions which exemplify the concurrence of a few major and distinctive categories of environment. Peru with its three zones of coastal plain, high mountains and interior forested lowlands; northern Canada with its forests and tundra and scattered mining communities; Egypt with its arid climate tempered by the waters of the Nile; Greece with its bare limestone uplands and fertile plains; Thailand with its forests and farm lands; each might be used as examples of different types of environments modified in various ways by the inhabitants or presenting difficulties of accessibility and development. Examples such as these can be used to introduce themes such as differing stages of economic development, differences in population densities, the importance of road, rail and waterways to trade and commerce. As with case-studies the countries or regions should be dealt with in considerable detail so that pupils become aware of the realities behind the generalisations.

The purposes of work of this kind are:

(a) to lay a secure foundation of training in using the sources on which the geographer builds his knowledge and perspectives;

(b) to ensure a regular use of atlas and globe so that the pupils become familiar with the distributions which they portray;

(c) to enable pupils to conjure up mental associations which give meaning to such terms as shifting agriculture, oil-field, fiord, savanna, Andes and irrigation and to give them confidence in using such terms;

(d) to build up general ideas or concepts involving sets of relationships, such as those implied in the term 'tropical forest' with its associations of climate, vegetation, primitive agriculture, possibilities of commercial products and the difficulties of land transport, disease and other developmental problems.

If the school can achieve these purposes in the earlier years of secondary education (which may include the later years of the Middle school) then pupils are well prepared for more exacting work at the later stages.

Before going on some thought must be given to the needs of the less able pupils. Much of the argument has assumed that pupils can be trained to use books, maps, pictures and statistics, and can comprehend the spoken word. It is the common experience of teachers that the kinds of materials with which they work present difficulties for some pupils, who become confused and frustrated by their failure to handle the tools of learning. There is a shortage of published material suitable for boys and girls who have difficulty with reading and simple arithmetic. This is no argument for excluding them from an active share in lessons. Some teachers prepare work cards on which pictures are mounted and a simply worded set of instructions are written. Some use three dimensional maps from which the relief is easily read; sometimes the pupils themselves have made the maps by cutting out the shapes of continents in hardboard and modelling the mountain ranges and plateaus on their flat surfaces. Their records of work may be in the form of models or drawings or may require a small amount of writing. Some teachers place the emphasis on the spoken word, which may be recorded on tape and used in conjunction with visual material. It is better to encourage such pupils to use whatever skills they possess rather than to exclude them from the process of finding out something for themselves; indeed a subject like geography often provides a strong motive for improving literacy, numeracy and map-reading. It is better that they should learn at a descriptive level something of the variety of life and landscape in the world rather than be engulfed in a torrent of words and explanations which they cannot comprehend.

In the later years of the secondary school most pupils are developing an interest in regional, national and world affairs and are ready to

Table 2

EXPORTS (1964 or 1965) IN £ MILLIONS

Country	Minerals							Crops and Animal Products															Tourism	Total Exports
	GOLD	COPPER	CRUDE OIL	IRON ORE	DIAMONDS	TIN	MANGANESE	COCOA	GROUNDNUTS	WOOL	COFFEE	MAIZE	PALM KERNELS	SUGAR	PALM OIL	SISAL	FRUIT	COTTON	RUBBER	TIMBER	TEA	FISH		
SIERRA LEONE	10			5	20			0·6			1·3		2·4											61
GHANA					7	15	5	68			0·7									12				113
NIGERIA			68					43	37				27		14				11	6				263
UGANDA		6									35							3			2			64
KENYA											14					4		16			6		8	47
TANZANIA					7						11					22		10						81
ZAMBIA		171																1						190
MALAWI																					3·3			12
S. AFRICA	298				43					58		44		17			36					52		793

conduct enquiries that go beyond simple relationships. These enquiries, many of which have been suggested in earlier chapters, may take the form of studies in regional and systematic geography or they may be concerned with topics which do not fall neatly into these categories. Sometimes the teacher may find it necessary to direct the work closely but it is important that the skills nurtured in earlier years should be used in independent work, that studies should draw on the concepts learned earlier, and that more complex ideas should be dealt with. As far as possible pupils should be encouraged to examine evidence in order to reach conclusions. On page 63 is part of a table of statistics used by a school as an introduction to regional studies. Space does not permit the complete table to be shown, but this extract will serve to demonstrate the method.

The number of questions raised by a table of this kind is vast.

Which countries export cocoa? rubber? palm-kernels? wool? sisal? Why are these exports confined to certain countries? Why does Nigeria have a larger range of crop exports than Sierra Leone or Ghana? Which countries benefit most from mineral exports? In what ways does South Africa differ from the other countries and why? Why is tourism well developed in Kenya? Are the total exports of each country proportional to their populations? If not what effects have exports on standards of living? Some of these questions are relatively easy to answer, others are more searching.

The pupils themselves might ask questions which arise from studying the table. They might be interested in the dominance of copper in the Zambian economy or the small trade of Malawi. There would be recourse to text-books, atlases, and articles, just as there would be if each country was studied separately, but there is a difference. The pupils are seeking the solution to problems and looking at a group of countries comparatively. Table 3 is equally suggestive of questions

Table 3

Country	Area (000s km²)	Population (millions)	Density of population per km²
BRAZIL	8512	88·2	10
BOLIVIA	1099	4·7	3
ARGENTINA	2777	23·6	8
CHILE	757	9·5	12
COLOMBIA	1139	19·8	17
ECUADOR	284	5·7	19
BELGIUM	31	9·6	314
NETHERLANDS	34	12·8	375
WEST GERMANY	248	58·3	233
UNITED KINGDOM	244	55·3	226
FRANCE	547	50·2	91

which not only require some study of the countries listed but also focus attention on the differences in the stage of development between South American and Western European countries.

Exercises based on an examination of data of this kind as well as encompassing regional studies help pupils to gain a sense of world perspective.

Pupils may be asked to read a text-book account of a country and then set out the kinds of questions which the text-book does not answer. A twelve-year-old girl who had read a chapter on Iraq asked 'What is life like for a girl of my age in Iraq? Does she have to wear a veil? Does she go to school? Is she allowed to play games with her friends?' It took the teacher some time to find references which provided the answers, but they opened up a new vista of life in a Moslem country.

The geography room should be looked upon as a resource centre, equipped in a way which enables pupils of all shades of ability to develop and use skills concerned with understanding man and his management of the various environments on the earth's surface. Whether geography is taught in its own right, or as part of a programme of integrated studies, it has its distinctive frames of reference and its special methods of work. For older pupils it should move beyond description of disparate parts and seek to provide a sense of world perspective. It should be concerned with solving problems of the environments which man has jointly created with nature. It should promote the sense of freedom that comes with understanding, and is a necessary condition of effective citizenship in its national or international sense.

'A man who is ignorant of the society in which he lives, who knows nothing of its place in the world and who has not thought about his place in it is not a free man though he has the vote.'[6]

---

[6] *Half Our Future* HMSO 1963.

7

Geography and Society

In University circles there are those who believe that human and physical geography are so dissimilar in their subject-matter and methodologies that they should be regarded as separate disciplines; indeed in many Universities abroad the separation of the branches is an accomplished fact. There are others who consider that one of the tasks of geography is to show how human activities are related to the physical settings in which they take place. A recent Council of Europe report[1] argues for a harmonization of natural sciences and human geography and claims that 'geography has now reached a degree of maturity and development enabling it to make a vigorous contribution to the development of human society'. The report takes the view that geography is concerned with 'spatial aspects of human activities and their setting', and as far as most school geography is concerned there are few, if any, teachers who would wish to regard human and physical geography as separate subjects. They generally take the view that the 'spatial aspects of human activities', that is the description and explanation of the location and distribution of certain kinds of human behaviour, is one of geography's main contributions to helping boys and girls to understand contemporary society at local, national and international level. They also take the view that to some extent widespread forms of human behaviour can not be wholly divorced from the physical setting in which they take place; physical features, climate and biogeography sometimes promote and sometimes constrain the aims of people and the ways in which they seek to achieve them.

There are many subjects in the school curriculum which are concerned with the study of human behaviour, notably history, religion, literature, art and music, as well as some newer subjects such as economics and sociology. Some of them are closely linked with geography and others only peripherally associated with it. No geographical treatment of Latin America would be complete without

---

[1] *The Teaching of Geography at University Level* J. Tricart, Harrap 1969.

some reference to three centuries of Spanish and Portuguese rule; the geography of industrial Britain cannot be dissociated from the history of the eighteenth and nineteenth centuries or the economic and political forces of the twentieth; religion has played, and continues to play, an important part in the Middle East and in India and Pakistan. Thus, in helping the pupils to understand how and why human activities vary from one place to another the geographer is concerned not solely with the influences of physical geography but also with forces generated by human society itself—social, cultural, economic and political—some of which may in varying degrees be a reflection of the physical environment. It is not easy to distinguish any universal rules which geographers employ in schools in determining the limits of their responsibilities for teaching pupils about societies; indeed opinion on this matter would differ greatly from one teacher to another. There would, however, be general agreement on certain issues. For example the economic life of a people, their diet, clothing and dwelling places, their modes of travel, their public buildings, and the physical appearance of the people themselves would all be regarded as worthy of study provided that they differed manifestly from their analogues in our own and other countries. It is doubtful whether a geography teacher in Britain would spend much time teaching his pupils that Canadians eat apples, bacon, beef, potatoes, bread and butter or that they live in houses containing furniture which is familiar to us; he might, however, dwell on the greater use of timber and central heating in Canadian houses. He might not expatiate on the diet of the French, but would draw attention to the importance of wine in the domestic economy. Contrast this with his consideration of parts of south-west Asia where the varying importance of rice, dates, barley, mutton and goat's milk in the diet, the mud-brick houses, the donkey and camel as means of transport, and the effect of the Moslem religion upon the daily rhythm of life and the style of clothing, would all be regarded as proper subject-matter. These examples point to one of the ways in which geography teachers select material—they deal with those characteristics which make countries or regions significantly different from others giving them an individuality or identity which may express itself both visually and in human behaviour. His task, however, does not end with mere description. It is not simply a matter of random choice or ingrained custom that houses, foods, beverages, clothing and agriculture vary from one place to another.

Climate and physical features greatly influence the behaviour of human societies, and even at an elementary level pupils may be led to appreciate how these two fundamental geographical factors still exert powerful influences in human affairs. It is still possible, despite the many adaptations that have come through selective breeding and new farming methods, to indicate the broad climatic limits within which, for example, wheat, rice, maize, cotton, sugar-cane, the vine and many other crops may be grown, or dairy-farming carried on. The great arid zones, the equatorial forests, and the harsher regions of the tundra and the high-latitude coniferous forest belts stand out on maps of population density as areas inimical to close settlement. So too do the high lands where terrain is difficult or the climatic effects of altitude are reinforced by distance from the equator; conversely highland areas within the tropics may prove more favourable to settlement than lowlands. One important contribution which geography teachers can make towards helping their pupils to understand human societies is to lead them to a knowledge of the distribution of climates and relief features on the earth's surface in relationship to the promise they bear and the problems they pose for habitation.

Here, however, the geographer treads on the dangerous ground of determinism. Physical geography is but one of the keys to understanding. Superimposed upon the patterns of physical features and climate are the resources of minerals; and superimposed upon the natural world are the genius of individuals and the will and capacity of people to exploit the potential of a region and to live with its hazards; to add one further complication different nations may choose to manage similar environments in different ways. Thus human geography is compounded of many ingredients that conduce to variety, which now, as in the past, attracts the interest of young and old. It is, however, not enough to know that one society is different from another; education is concerned with helping pupils to understand why differences occur and this involves some grasp of social, political and economic matters. Two other important issues arise. The first is that life is everywhere changing its pace and quality, and school geography, if it is to be of any value to young people after they have left school, should be as much concerned with changes and the forces that generate them as with the present condition of peoples. Secondly, there are many points of similarity between one place and another; sometimes the similarities are deeply rooted in the physical world and sometimes in economic, cultural and political forces which operate over large areas; sometimes they reflect seemingly universal aspects of human behaviour the distributional implications of which it is a main purpose of theoretical geography to explore. The following sections deal with some of the large issues which should concern geographers in helping boys and girls to understand their world, particularly as they approach school-leaving age.

Differentials in Wealth

It is all too easy to ignore differentials in wealth in school geography. Most of the pupils in fourth and fifth forms can understand what is implied by the terms National Income or Gross National Product, particularly if they are simply regarded as indicating what is available for personal expenditure, government expenditure and investment expenditure. At an elementary level they can be introduced by comparing diets, clothing, homes and styles of life with our own. A more searching analysis of the terms may be of value in Sixth Form studies. The World Bank Atlas (1968),[2] from which figures in Table 4 are taken, throw a great deal of light on the comparative poverty of many nations and help boys and girls to understand how difficult it is for them to set up the infrastructure of education and a supply of capital which is necessary for economic growth. A starting point might be the per capita GNP figures for selected countries:

Table 4: *Per capita G.N.P.*

(All figures are in U.S. dollars, refer to 1967, and are rounded up to the nearest $10.)

Some affluent countries

USA	3670
CANADA	2380
AUSTRALIA	1970
NEW ZEALAND	1890
SWEDEN	2500
FRANCE	1960
WEST GERMANY	1750
UNITED KINGDOM	1700

For most African countries the per capita GNP figures are below $150 but some exceptions are:

ZAMBIA	180
RHODESIA	230
LIBERIA	190
GHANA	200
SOUTH AFRICA	590

A good many Asiatic countries have figures below $200; the range includes:

---

[2] The limitations of the figures for Gross National Product are also explained.

F

INDIA	90
The PHILIPPINES	180
MALAYSIA	290
SINGAPORE	600
JAPAN	1000

South American examples are:

BOLIVIA	170
COLOMBIA	300
PERU	350
CHILE	470
ARGENTINA	800
VENEZUELA	880

The following examples from Southern Europe and the Middle East pose interesting questions:

BULGARIA	690
GREECE	700
SPAIN	680
UNITED ARAB REPUBLIC (Egypt)	160
SYRIA	180
SAUDI ARABIA	350
LIBYA	720
ISRAEL	1200
KUWAIT	3490

Figures such as these may be visually presented by pupils in the form of histograms. They not only present a startling picture of the uphill task of many countries, where the total available income may be less than a country like Britain spends annually on education and welfare services, but they also provide starting points for enquiries by pupils. The importance of mineral wealth for example, in countries like Kuwait, Libya (which has increased its per capita National Income tenfold in a decade), Venezuela and Zambia is striking. Articles in the Current Affairs series of the Geographical Magazine give accounts of some of the improvements that follow when countries have surplus goods to sell. Foreign aid programmes take on a greater significance in the light of figures such as these presented above.

Problems of Tropical and Arid Lands
Special treatment of tropical and arid lands is justified if only because the areas are so extensive and are generally associated with low standards of living. In his classical work on 'The Tropical

World' Pierre Gourou significantly starts his survey with accounts of the low densities of population in many areas and the prevalence of disease—malaria, intestinal diseases of many kinds, river blindness, yaws, tropical ulcers, yellow fever, sleeping-sickness and malnutrition, to name a few. The World Health Organisation publishes accounts of the work of special teams and points the need for more extensive medical and hygiene services and better balanced diets. Primitive cultivation, fertilization by means of burning bush and foliage, avoidance of deep digging lest soil erosion follows, are all ways of making the best use of soils prone to heavy leaching and vulnerable to surface run-off after heavy rain. Massive research on soil management, the improvement of health services, the exploitation of forest resources, the establishment of plantation agriculture, the installation of hydro-electric power schemes, the building of roads, railways and ports, all require capital resources which are difficult to come by. Many of the exports—rubber, vegetable oils, cocoa and cane-sugar—are vulnerable to competition in world markets. Industrial developments, which are essential if standards of living are to be raised, are thus inhibited. Boys and girls who have not understood these widespread problems are unlikely to gain a proper sympathy for other peoples. Studies can be made of the ways in which countries such as Liberia, Zambia, Malaysia, Ghana and parts of Brazil have progressed in the uphill struggle to improve the lot of their peoples in the face of difficult tropical environments.

The problems of the 'Utilization and Human Geography of Deserts' have been set forth by Professor Dresch[3] who points out that nomadic pastoralism as a way of life is declining. The dry areas tend to become emptier; the pressure on the semi-arid margins grows as farmers encroach upon them from moister areas with improved methods of dry cultivation and nomads seek the better pastures which they can afford. Over-grazing and over-cultivation are pressing dangers. As population pressure grows the need to irrigate land wherever water can be supplied becomes more urgent. To the ancient irrigation works of the Middle East must be added more expensive schemes such as those installed in Pakistan, India, the USA, the USSR and Egypt. The importance of minerals, particularly petroleum, to a number of arid countries is demonstrated by reference to their effects upon the national prosperity mentioned in an earlier section of this chapter.

Technology
An increasing part in shaping the nature and quality of life is played by technology. At a humble level the transistor radio which may now

---

[3] *Institute of British Geographers Transactions* No. 40. December 1966.

be heard in the bazaars of East Africa and India or villages in the Orinoco Lowlands breaks the isolation of communities, exposing them to means of mass communication and propaganda. Agricultural technology may extend the margins of cultivation as it has done significantly in the lands growing wheat in Canada, cotton in USA or barley in Finland. The application of fertilisers and the use of new strains of seed are beginning to transform the agriculture of India; within a decade the production of food-stuffs, which had remained relatively stable for many years, has been raised by over 40 per cent, affording prospects of economic and social benefits undreamt of a generation ago. The remarkable progress of British agriculture through the use of fertilisers, machinery and rationalisation has enabled less than 4 per cent of the labour force to produce some 60 per cent of food requirements in a region whose northern margins approach the limits of cultivation. In many countries increased efficiency in agriculture is a fundamental prerequisite to economic and social improvements, for workers released from the land may ultimately become available for productive work in other spheres—in mining, industrial production, transport and social services which raise the level of life from mere economic subsistence to affluence, the enjoyment of recreations and the pursuit of cultural activities; the process of change may, however, be slow and painful. Cipolla[4] describes the disparities between nations as they existed in 1950, and the situation may be brought up-to-date by reference to the Statistical Yearbooks of the United Nations. Broadly speaking the 'developed countries' of the world have 20 per cent or fewer of their working populations engaged in agriculture while in the less developed countries the figures may rise to between 50 and 90 per cent. Thus the improvement of agriculture is the first step towards a richer style of life.

Great achievements in building and engineering are no new thing. The ancient irrigation works of the Euphrates-Tigris lowlands and Persia, Hindu, Greek and Aztec temples, Roman roads and aqueducts, European mediaeval churches, and the terraced rice-fields, of south-east Asia all testify to a long history of boldly conceived and skilfully executed works carried out with relatively simple tools and materials. Modern technology is distinguished by its complexity, its scale and the rate at which it can change the environment and human activities. It is, too, frequently expensive; one of the great problems of poorer nations is to amass the capital needed to achieve what has been sometimes referred to as an 'economic breakthrough', the point at which the benefits of applied capital begin significantly to improve living

---

[4] *The Economic History of World Population* Penguin 1962.

standards. In countries with large populations such as India and China the scale of investment in heavy industry, engineering, textiles, chemicals and transport must be very large before substantial benefits can accrue. In countries with 'advanced' economies the effects of cumulative applications of technology and planning increase wealth and alter the character of the environment at a rapid rate. Thus technology becomes a major geographical factor.

Numerous articles have been written on this theme. Changes in ships and shipping[5] have influenced the siting of heavy industries using bulk imported materials; coastal locations with deep water access are increasingly sought by iron and steel works, oil refineries, and petro-chemical industries; container ships not only alter the character of ports but threaten to reduce the number required in densely peopled countries with good internal communications. A generation ago Professor E. G. R. Taylor wrote a slim pamphlet on 'The Geography of an Air Age',[6] since that time the growth of traffic in passengers and goods, the development of internal and international air routes and airports, and the pressing problems of sites for new airports and rapid communications between them and city centres have become important issues in modern geography. The railway, at one time the main artery of land transport in much of the world, now competes with the motorway. Developments in transport involve not only a fresh approach to questions of location; they also modify our ideas of distance. In some circumstances time or cost may be more important than the number of miles travelled. Interesting exercises have been carried out in some schools in map transformations which represent distance as time or cost; the resultant distortion of traditional maps vividly reveals the degrees of remoteness or accessibility which may exist between places. Similarly, studies of road networks promote an understanding of the efficiency and density of communications and permit comparisons to be made between one area and another. Radio and tele-communications present another field of investigation for geographers. The Post Office tower in London is not just an interesting architectural feature; it is symbolic of the electronic revolution which has impressed itself upon the surface of countries like Britain in radar stations and broadcasting transmission stations. The siting of these stations and the delimitation of broadcasting regions in Britain are firmly rooted in geography.

---

[5] See S. H. Beaver in *Geography* No. 235 April 1967 and G. Manners on Transport Costs and Freight Rates and the Changing Economic Geography of Iron Ore in *Geography* No. 236 July 1967.

[6] Published by the Royal Institute of International Affairs 1945.

One other aspect of technology may be mentioned here. The production and harnessing of power for industrial and domestic purposes is a common topic in school geography. It is less common, however, for pupils to see the impact of power production in a world setting. J. P. Cole[7] has used the per capita consumption of energy as one of the indicators by means of which levels of development between countries may be compared. The following selected figures, which are given in kilograms of coal equivalent for the year 1959, reinforce other themes suggested in this chapter which throw light on problems of development. United Kingdom 4590, Sweden 3000, France 2370, Argentina 1033, Peru 315, Malaya 240, Burma 50, India 145, Morocco 135. These figures in isolation can be misleading, but coupled with other information they help pupils to appreciate the extent to which economic and social conditions vary from one country to another.

Urbanisation

One of the consequences of the technological revolution has been the remarkable growth of large cities and urban agglomerations. It is commonly stated that the population of Britain is 80 per cent urban and 20 per cent rural. This distinction conceals the fact that the rural element is essentially urban-orientated, depending for goods and services on the towns. A town such as Dingwall, with a population of 4000, is closely linked with remote communities in Ross and Cromarty spread over a radius of more than forty miles. In turn Dingwall and other towns of its size look to Inverness for a wider range of services. In a sense it can be claimed that Britain is a wholly urban country. This interlocking of town and country, which finds expression in the city-region concept and in the Redcliffe-Maud proposals for the reform of local government, is a common characteristic of developed countries.

As urbanisation and communications have developed it has become apparent that the study of settlement patterns, urban functions and the morphology of towns and cities is essential if boys and girls are to understand the nature of the environments in which they live and the purposes of planning.[8] It is equally important for them to realise that the characteristics, advantages and problems of urban settlement are not unique to Britain but are shared by many other

---

[7] *The Geography of World Affairs* Penguin 3rd Edition 1964.

[8] R. E. Dickinson *The City Region in Western Europe* Routledge and Kegan Paul 1967. Everson & Fitzgerald *Settlement Patterns* Longmans 1969.

countries.[9] Schools are increasingly turning their attention to field-work in towns and villages. Shopping centres, traffic flows, industrial, commercial and residential zones may be studied on the ground. Broader questions require reference to maps, statistics and other sources of information. Games and theoretical models may also be used to stimulate an awareness of the growth, shapes and functions of towns and the hierarchies of settlement that exist.

In this chapter a number of broad themes have been suggested which help pupils to look at human geography in its world setting. They are essentially more appropriate to older than to younger pupils, and the vocabularies and relationships which they embrace can only be based upon a foundation of empirical studies of human activities and societies.

Every geography teacher could suggest other general topics which could be added, such as multi-racial societies, religious differences, international political associations, conservation and the pollution of the environment. All are concerned with forces that influence human affairs; some are more complex than others, but most are within the power of comprehension of older boys and girls if their programme has included well chosen studies of small communities and countries which widely represent the variety of conditions in which people live.

One of the weaknesses of school geography has been that the general relationships upon which regional geography has depended for some sort of order have been mainly chosen from the relatively stable fields of physical geography. In a limited sense valid comparisons may be made, by reference to these elements, between Manchuria and the St. Lawrence Valley, between the tropical grasslands of Northern Australia and those of West Africa, or between Algeria and Southern California. But until considerations of race, history, national income, stage of development and the like are taken into account there can be little hope of giving pupils a satisfying insight into the complexities of the world. Examples such as these illustrate the need for a more thoughtful treatment of economic, social and cultural affairs in human geography. Once pupils have grasped the significance of these matters they can apply a more accurate frame of reference to the study of their own and other countries.

If geographers were asked to give a single justification for teaching about human societies it would probably rest on the need for international understanding. This grows from an understanding of the

---

[9] P. Hall *The World Cities* Weidenfeld & Nicholson 1966 and E. Jones *Towns and Cities* Oxford University Press 1966.

home environment, and the ways in which other communities differ from, or are similar to, our own. 'By rendering a better understanding of the exact nature of man's relation to his surroundings and by pointing out the immense influence of culture, geography suggests that there is nothing fixed and rigid in that relation and that it can be modified in a way that is favourable to man.'[10]

---

[10] Pierre Gourou *The Tropical World* Longmans 1954.

8

Geography, Science and Mathematics

School geography deals with many topics which depend upon a knowledge of elementary science and mathematics; in turn it may provide data and problems which interest teachers of science and mathematics. A random selection of topics chosen from standard text-books of geography would include the following examples:

Geomorphology: chemistry of rocks and minerals; solution and precipitation; porosity; freezing and regelation; hydrology; processes of weathering; sedimentation.

Meteorology and climatology: temperature; barometric pressure; humidity; evaporation and condensation; dew point; convection; cloud-formation; lapse-rates; the water-cycle.

Oceanography: salinity; density; convection currents; plankton and food chains.

Biogeography: soils; plant associations; habitats.

Mathematics: graphical representation; co-ordinates (grid references); gradients; two-dimensional representation of three-dimensional features; sections; latitude and longitude; map projections; statistics.

In an infinitely flexible curriculum the science and mathematics that the geographer needs would be taught by his colleagues at the right time. In many schools consultation between departments takes place to achieve as much synchronisation as possible, but progression in the separate subjects does not always permit ideal solutions and the geographer may be obliged, at times, to introduce his pupils to a little science and, more rarely, mathematics, to deal with immediate needs. However his concern is not so much with the physics, chemistry and biology of the elements with which he deals but with certain spatial relationships that exist among them. Moreover the elements that he seeks to describe and explain in their inter-relationships are not solely drawn from the fields of the natural sciences but include aspects of human behaviour. The exponents of a modern approach to school geography advocate a more scientific attitude towards both physical and human geography and a greater use of mathematics and statistics than would have been thought appropriate as recently as ten years ago, and this chapter is devoted to the implications of some recent developments. What are the arguments for this change in outlook?

First it is claimed that regional studies, the heart of modern geography, have concentrated on demonstrating that each region is a unique combination of a group of forces which intermingle in different proportions from place to place. The basic forces were shown diagrammatically by the late Sir Dudley Stamp in the form of a semi-circle with Man at the centre,[1] indicating the relationship between man and his environment. A slightly more elaborate

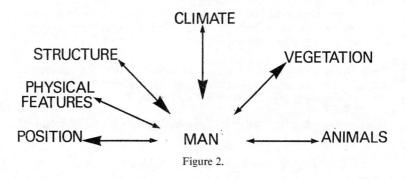

Figure 2.

arrangement is revealed by the widespread practice of organising regional geography in schools in the sequence—position, geology, physical features, climate, natural vegetation, soils, agriculture, industry, towns, communications. There is a recognisable logic in the order; and for the examination candidate the sequence provides a useful check-list when a region is to be described or one region compared with another. The purpose of the exercise is to explain how variations in each separate ingredient in the mixture produces the individuality of each region, that is to say it is concerned with establishing the basis for 'areal differentiation'. At the same time the method is useful for comparing areas which have certain features in common—for example the Baltic and Laurentian Shields, the Alps and Himalayas, or Temperate Grasslands of Argentina and Australia —but which differ from one another in other respects. In spite of its

---

[1] *Applied Geography* Penguin 1960.

virtues this treatment of regional geography is criticised on the following grounds:

(a) By emphasising the uniqueness of each area it depends largely on memorisation because it lacks a sufficient framework of general concepts.

(b) It leads to a stereotyped treatment in which undue weight may be given to irrelevancies.

(c) It omits from the reckoning many factors (such as those outlined in the previous chapter) which greatly affect human geography.

(d) It fails to demonstrate many of the similarities that exist over wide areas of the earth's surface.

(e) It presupposes that valid boundaries may be drawn around regions of a multi-functional character.[2] The idea of a fixed region may be contrasted with this definition of a region given by a British geographer:[3] 'A region is an area in which selected phenomena interact significantly. The selection of . . . phenomena and the degrees of interaction to be established as significant are matters for the individual geographer'.

Secondly, it is argued that traditional geography is prone to vague statements based on general impressions when better tools of analysis would lead to greater precision. At a very simple level this can be illustrated by the statements 'Canada is the world's most important producer of nickel', 'Jamaica is the world's greatest producer of bauxite' and 'Australia has more sheep than any other country in the world'. An examination of the statistics shows that in recent years Canada produced between 60 and 70 per cent of the world's nickel and Jamaica about 25 per cent of its bauxite, while Australia has some 15 per cent of the world's sheep. The degree of dominance, concealed in superlatives but revealed by more precise analysis, is more significant than the fact of dominance. Many examples of unquantified vague statements will occur to the teacher. It is commonly stated of South Wales that the decline of coal-mining has resulted in a good deal of commuting between the older mining towns and the developing areas to the South and East. An analysis of 'The Journey to Work in South Wales'[4] expressed as the absolute numbers of people involved and the proportions they represent of the working population of each district, and recorded in maps,

---

[2] See Kimble *The Inadequacy of the Regional Concept, London Essays in Geography* Ed Stamp and Wooldridge: Longmans Green 1951.

[3] Professor E. Bowen (in a lecture at Oxford 1969).

[4] G. Humphrys: Institute of British Geographers, *Transactions No. 36* June 1965.

provides a good example for Sixth Form pupils of how the nature and scale of the commuting can be shown quantitatively. Earlier pages of this pamphlet contain examples of ways in which, even among primary school children, descriptive words like 'a lot' (applied to traffic flow) or 'hot' (applied to temperature) can be stated numerically and thus permit comparisons to be made between one place and another or one occasion and another. When, however, relationships between phenomena are expressed with greater precision techniques which require more than simple counting and measuring are required. Some examples, in 'New Ways in Geography' Book 2[5] relate distance and time, height and rainfall, slope and potato yields. The use of a simple grid for storing data is demonstrated by W. V. Tidswell in his 'Severn Bridge Accessibility' exercise in which the road distances between selected towns around the Severn estuary before and after the opening of the Severn Bridge are recorded and analysed. Other techniques involving regression and statistical methods of correlation are referred to later in this chapter.

Thirdly, growing out of the rejection of a stereotyped regionalism and the demand for greater precision, is the search for law and order, backed by scientific method. Whitehead[6] defines the notion of Law as 'some measure of regularity or persistence or recurrence . . . an essential element in the urge towards technology, methodology, scholarship and speculation'. He also distinguishes between scholarship, based on exact observation and logic, and speculation, both of which are necessary for progress in knowledge. There may be many opinions about what is meant by 'scientific method' in secondary schools. N. Booth[7] has suggested that it means 'learning to make observations with a conscious looking for patterns of behaviour and, when a pattern is detected, the search for an explanation'. Geographers would not dispute these general ideas, even though there is a difference between the 'closed systems' involved in a great deal of laboratory science and the 'open systems' which concern the geographer. In laboratory science the operator controls the elements with which he deals so as to exclude or minimise those which are irrelevant. For the geographer no such control is possible; he works in an open system in which the study of a few variables can never be wholly detached from other variables, some of which may be known and measurable and some of which may be due to chance factors. If we return to Whitehead's definition of Law a great deal of Law can

---

[5] Cole and Beynon: Blackwell 1968.
[6] *Adventure of Ideas* Penguin 1933.
[7] *Trends in Education* No. 17, January 1970.

be expected to exist in the realm of physical geography, but it is also true that 'some measure of regularity' can be detected in human and regional geography. Modern geography is concerned with discovering and explaining pattern and recurrence, and since the first step in the process is accurate observation and recording the need for greater precision is evident. But the scientific process does not end there. The advancement of knowledge calls for 'speculation', that is the development of theory to explain pattern and recurrence. Theory, once formulated, must be tested against reality. The 'Laws' that are to be found in human geography differ from many of those in physical science in that they are less precise; the statistical probability of recurrence is lower because of the impact of many variables. Nevertheless if the probability of recurrence is high then it is claimed that they can be used to predict. The term 'predict' appears to be used in two senses. In the first place it can mean foretelling events. An example of this is provided by a simulation exercise concerned with the growth of a town based on information about the existing road pattern, the amenity values of the area, zones unfavourable to housing development and the like. If a map of the existing town and its surrounding area is covered by a grid each square can be assigned a first probability rating for future development and a sequence in the development programme. To incorporate chance factors it is necessary to employ random numbers which select additions to the first probability ratings produced from known factors. Thus if a number of pupils carry out this exercise they will arrive at different answers in detail, but their maps will show a considerable degree of agreement. Diffusion exercises which attempt to show how, for example, a new idea in farming or in hygiene may be spread in a scattered community carry the same meaning for the word 'predict'. The word may, however, be used in the sense of predicating; in this sense, given a certain amount of information about a place or phenomenon, the geographer may, by applying 'Laws', make further statements which have a high probability of being correct. In this case his 'prediction' may be immediately tested against the reality. For example given a certain amount of information about the size of a town and the distribution and sizes of nearby towns it is possible to state with some certainty the range of goods and services which it is likely to offer, though the unusual (such as the number of antique shops in Bury St. Edmunds)[8] might evade the 'predictor'. The scientific approach should also give the pupils tools and methods for solving problems since, like prediction, the testing of theory is a problem-solving exercise. The difference between a traditional approach to geography and the newer approach is not that the

---

[8] Everson and Fitzgerald, op cit.

Traditional Approach

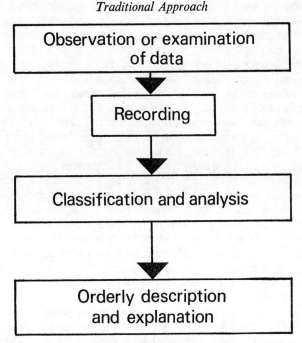

Figure 3.

former was 'unscientific', but that it tended to stop short the scientific method before it reached the stage of speculation or theory. This may be illustrated in diagrammatic form in Figs. 3 and 4.

Models

One of the inevitable consequences of the search for pattern is the development of models of thinking. Haggett[9] has written 'Models are made necessary by the complexity of reality. They are a conceptual prop to our understanding, and as such provide for the teacher a simplified and rational picture for the classroom, and for the researcher a source of working hypotheses to test against reality. Models convey not the whole truth but a useful and comprehensible part of it.' The term 'model', as used here, does not refer to every form of simplification of reality. The custom of dividing a country into regions by drawing lines on a map is a device for simplifying reality; but this kind of simplification applies solely to the country

[9] *Locational Analysis in Human Geography* Arnold 1965.

New Approach

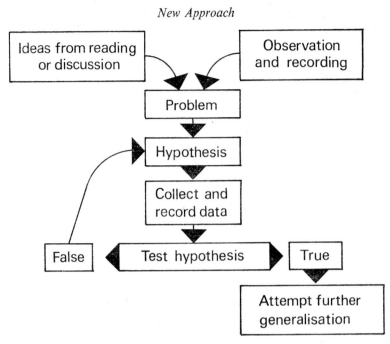

Figure 4.

concerned and cannot be transferred to other countries, for each has its own set of divisions and sub-divisions, which are not repeated elsewhere. The essence of models is that they deal with concepts, that is relationships which recur. The model is a simplified statement—often in diagrammatic form—which depicts the general features of a relationship. Against it any specific example may be tested. While the model is broadly true of the relationships depicted a specific case may reveal one or more distortions of the model. A valuable exercise in geography is to identify the nature and amount of the distortions and to explain them. Models introduced at stages when pupils can appreciate them are valuable conceptual frameworks. Their use as measuring devices for the real world is a reversal of the empirical approach in which the study of a number of real examples is used inductively to arrive at generalisations. The admixture of the two methods is a feature of modern geography teaching; the empirical approach has a much greater place with younger children and models with older pupils; but at no stage in school geography can either method be regarded as unsuitable once the pupil begins to display powers of reasoning.

In physical geography teachers have made use of models for many years. A small selection only is quoted here, and the examples are usually portrayed in diagrams accompanied by notes.

River valleys—upper, middle and lower courses; profiles
Scarpland topography
Residual mountain topography with accordant summits
Features of glacial erosion and deposition
Faults, rift valleys and horsts
Bjerknes' model of a depression
Rainshadow
Herbertson's 'natural regions'
Soil catena

All are useful tools of thinking and can be widely applied to assist the understanding of reality; the real situations which they simplify frequently contain distortional elements which call for explanation. For example, the presence of hard and soft bands of rock may modify considerably an 'ideal' valley profile, a tract of savanna may be crossed by broad bands of dense forest in well-watered valley bottoms, and a rainshadow effect may be nullified temporarily by divergencies from 'prevailing' weather conditions.

In human geography models have not been used on the same scale, but developments in the subject suggest that they can increasingly find a place in the classroom, providing general frameworks of reference. A sequential model showing stages of development in the British iron-and-steel industry might be constructed as a basis of comparison to explain locations and stages of development in other countries (Fig. 5). The symbols used for a simple model are as shown in Figure 5.

Stage 1 (as represented by the Wealden and Forest of Dean industries) and Stage 2 are of historical interest only in Britain but examples of the second stage exist in China. Stage 4 is represented at such places as Ebbw Vale and Consett. Most of the large plants in Britain are represented in Stages 5 and 6. Parallels with all of these stages (with the possible exception of Stage 1) are to be found throughout the world. The later stages show the increasing importance of large plants with advanced technologies, large markets, and efficient and low-cost transport.

A consideration of the needs of town-dwellers can be used by older pupils to construct theoretical models of a town in which housing can be related to industry, commerce, shopping, recreation, education, medical and social services, recreation and transport. New towns in Britain are practical examples of models applied to specific situations which require modifications (or distortions) of the 'ideal'

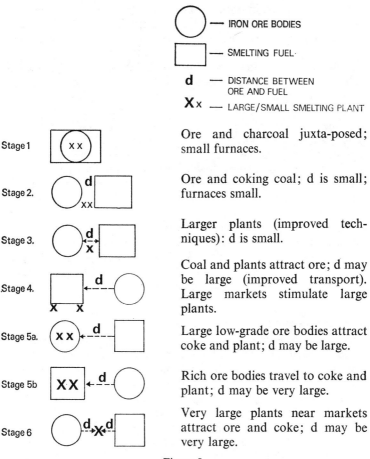

Figure 5.

Stage 1 — Ore and charcoal juxta-posed; small furnaces.

Stage 2. — Ore and coking coal; d is small; furnaces small.

Stage 3. — Larger plants (improved techniques): d is small.

Stage 4. — Coal and plants attract ore; d may be large (improved transport). Large markets stimulate large plants.

Stage 5a. — Large low-grade ore bodies attract coke and plant; d may be large.

Stage 5b — Rich ore bodies travel to coke and plant; d may be very large.

Stage 6 — Very large plants near markets attract ore and coke; d may be very large.

model. Pupils may compare their home town and nearby towns and thus arrive at some understanding of the purpose of urban renewal and the restrictions under which re-development is carried out.

Among the theoretical models which have profoundly influenced the work of human geographers in recent years pride of place must be given to Von Thunens' system of land use[10] and Christaller's work on 'Central Places in Southern Germany'.[11] Both have

[10] English translation *Von Thunen's Isolated State* P. Hall 1966. See also Chisholm *Rural Settlement and Land Use* Hutchinson 1967.
[11] See also R. E. Dickinson *The City Region in Western Europe* Routledge 1967.

G

stimulated research into locational studies in human geography, the results of which are increasingly being felt in schools. The steady growth of games and simulation exercises, which incorporate many of the features of theoretical models, is likely to afford a source of interest and innovation for teachers in schools. Simple games may well provide situations in which less able pupils are actively engaged in manipulating data in a way which leads to understanding relationships which would be difficult to convey by traditional methods of teaching. Past experience of teaching by means of models in physical geography suggests that while they have great value their use is not without dangers. Sometimes models have been taught as a substitute for reality; sometimes they have introduced too early in the course, ideas that are too vast for young children to comprehend; sometimes they have been stretched beyond their usefulness; some have been taught without an experiential basis which gives meaning to the vocabulary and elements involved. Wisely used they can transfer some of the burden of learning from unrelieved memorisation to reasoning within orderly systems of relationships. If they are to be effective the pupils should participate in both the construction of models and their testing against reality.

Mathematics and Statistics

This section deals with some applications of mathematics and statistics to geography without attempting a detailed treatment. Counting and measuring, and various methods of recording data collected in this way, are already familiar to geography teachers. As new developments in school mathematics become more widely practised it is important that the geography teacher should be aware of them and of their usefulness as tools in his subject. The fear of mathematics that some teachers entertain can often be dispelled by consultation with colleagues in the mathematical department, many of whom are interested in geography and in the data and problems with which geography is concerned. The main arguments for a greater use of mathematics in geography can be briefly stated.

1   Patterns can be revealed by mathematical techniques that cannot be detected by a subjective study, for example 'nearest neighbour analysis' to analyse settlement patterns.

2   When modern techniques are applied to old problems the answers achieved provide more precise and convincing demonstrations than were previously possible.

3   New approaches, particularly in diffusion of ideas or people, central place studies and agriculture have revealed new knowledge.

What kinds of mathematics are likely to be used in school geography? A brief summary is given here but for a full account the reader is referred to text-books such as that by Cole and King[12] and S. Gregory.[13]

Statistics

1 can help to sample a total 'population' (the number of items) and avoid the necessity of studying all the data;

2 combined with mathematical techniques help to store selected information in an easy and logical way until it is needed again;

3 can test the validity of many statements (inferential statistics) by assessing the probability that two samples belong to the same population;

4 can summarise data so that they can be more easily understood (descriptive statistics);

5 can help in generalising and creating further models or theories;

6 can help towards an assessment of trends, sometimes through graphical approaches.

There are various reasons why samples should be used; it may be necessary to save time, there may be too few enumerators, the population may be too large to count (eg the journeys to work in a region), or some of the information may be unknown or inaccessible (eg temperatures over Britain on a given day).

Three common methods of devising a sample are:

(a) a random sample may be made by using random numbers to select the items;

(b) a structured sample involves firm adherence to certain rules of selection. (For example in a survey of building materials every tenth house in each street could be recorded; or items might be divided into classes such as arable, permanent grass, moorland and a strict proportion of each examined.);

(c) a judgment sample may be used when one area is taken to represent all similar areas in the country with respect to a specific piece of information.

The degree of certainty required will decide the size of the sample; if we wish to assess a population measure with confidence limits of 95 per cent, a simple calculation which is shown in standard text-books will indicate the size of the sample required.

[12] *Quantitative Geography* Wiley 1968.
[13] *Statistical Methods and the Geographer*, Longmans. 2nd Ed. 1968.

Graphs, tables and histograms are used to store information. The grid, (or matrix), commonly used in motoring handbooks to show distances between towns, can be applied to other situations. For example agricultural activities such as dairy farming, cereal cultivation, permanent pasture, sugar-beet cultivation in a group of farms could be recorded in a grid (Fig. 6) in which 1 indicates presence and 0 absence.

Farming Activity		A	B	C	D	E
Farm	1	1	1	1	0	0
''	2	1	1	1	1	1
''	3	0	1	1	1	0
''	4	0	0	0	0	1
''	5	0	0	1	1	1
''	6	0	1	1	0	1

Figure 6.

In descriptive statistics the mean, mode and median are means of calculating average situations, and variance (which describes the spread of the data about the mean) involves an understanding of standard deviations and the interquartile range.

Two main types of test are used in inferential statistics. The first are concerned with establishing whether differences between sets of data are likely to be the result of chance or whether they indicate significant differences between the sets of data. The second are designed to establish the degrees of correlation that exist between two sets of data. Spearman's rank correlation test is relatively easy to apply to many situations which occur in school geography.

Set theory has a number of simple applications to geography particularly in the form of Venn diagrams. A simple example which vividly shows the relationships between stock, arable and mixed farming is given in Fig. 7.

Similarly major economic activities of the countries of North Africa and the Middle East—agriculture, nomadic pastoralism and oil

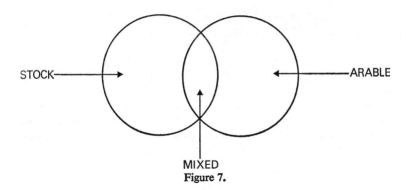

MIXED
Figure 7.

production—could be demonstrated as in Fig. 8. (Note: where an activity is of minor significance, such as oil in Egypt or nomadism in Iraq, it has been ignored.)

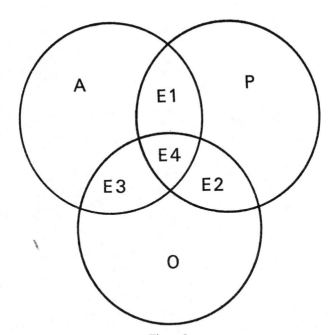

Figure 8.

Universal set—countries of North Africa and Middle East.

Set A—agriculture	E1 = AP: Egypt, Morrocco, Sudan
Set P—nomadic pastoralism	E2 = PO: Kuwait, Saudi Arabia, Libya
Set O—oil production	E3 = AO: Iraq
	E4 = APO: Algeria

When the number of sub-sets is large the information may be more conveniently read from a simple grid.

Regression analysis can be widely used in school geography to show how one variable may be related to another. Scatter diagrams are frequently constructed by younger pupils in the science laboratories of secondary schools to show how an increase in one variable is accompanied by an increase or decrease in another. In Table 5 the height above sea level and the mean annual rainfall for seventeen stations in South Wales are recorded.

Table 5

Station	Height (metres)	Rainfall (millimetres)
1	20	910
2	42	1020
3	55	1260
4	60	860
5	61	1060
6	140	1040
7	170	1130
8	185	1480
9	225	1410
10	232	1410
11	262	1620
12	275	1460
13	330	1670
14	340	1780
15	350	1470
16	415	1920
17	455	1970

Figure 9 shows the scatter diagram recording height and rainfall. The broken line is a roughly drawn line indicating regression of rainfall on height. To assist in drawing it, one fixed point recording the mean height and rainfall can be inserted, and the line made to pass through it. More refined methods could be used to construct an accurate regression line and lines which indicate the coefficient of correlation between height and rainfall. These are described in standard text-books. For most school purposes they are unnecessary. A reasonably accurate line can be inserted by eye without calculating the mean and it shows that, in general, an increase in height of 100 m corresponds to an increase in rainfall of about 250 mm. Wide divergencies from the mean, such as those

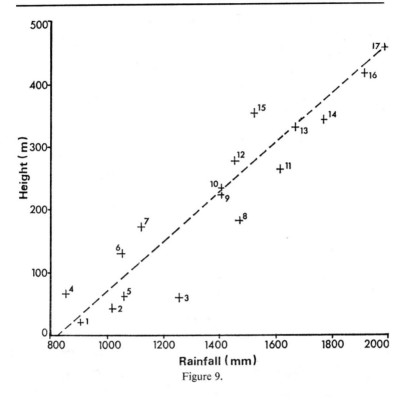

Figure 9.

revealed by stations 3 and 15 indicate the effects of exposure, shelter and other extraneous factors which cannot be excluded in 'open systems' as they can under laboratory conditions. It is possible to use regression techniques on data which will produce curved lines and also on data involving more than two variables. Sometimes data which produce curves can be replotted on logarithmic graph paper to produce straight lines.

Geometries

Geometry plays an increasing part in modern geography. Christaller's hexagons, Lewis's shore-line curves, the exponential curves of river profiles, and curves of erosion surfaces are examples.

Topological maps merit special mention. A familiar topological map is that of the London Underground Railways in which the relative positions of stations are preserved but distance and detailed changes of direction are omitted. Mention has already been made in Chapter 4 of map transformations in which geographic distance has been replaced by other measures of distance such as time and cost of journeys. If a map of Britain is drawn in which counties are retained

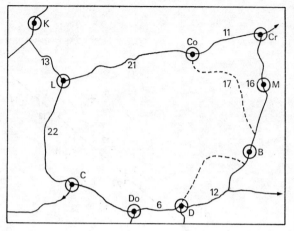

Figure 10.

Distances shown in km.
Broken lines denote B class roads.

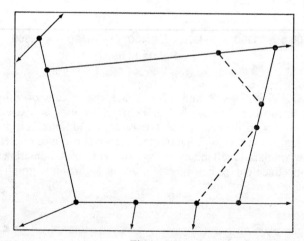

Figure 11.

in their relative positions but their areas are replaced by their populations the economic dominance of the Metropolitan–Midland–Merseyside axis is vividly portrayed.

The study of road networks normally involves simple topological transformations. Figure 10 shows the road network (A and B class roads only) in a part of Scotland covering an area of about 1200 square km (480 square miles). Distance between settlements are shown in km. Figure 11 shows a topological map of the same portion of the network. Using the 'nodes' and 'edges' it is possible to calculate a coefficient of integration (or connectivity) between settlements in the area shown; this indicates the number of alternative routes that exist. The efficiency of the network can be calculated by comparing straight-line distances between settlements with actual road distances. The density can be calculated by the mileage of roads for the given area.[14] In this instance the coefficients of integration, efficiency and density are low. Similar exercises carried out in rural Lincolnshire and the industrial West Riding would produce higher coefficients and permit precisely defined comparisons to be made. An examination of contrasting road networks might be used as an introduction to the study of highlands, agricultural lowlands and industrial regions in Britain. For less able pupils the more complicated calculations might be omitted.

Gravity models derive their name from Newton's law of gravitation which states that every particle of matter in the universe attracts every other particle with a force whose direction is that of the line joining the two and whose magnitude is directly proportional to the product of the masses divided by the square of their distance from each other. This is summed up in the equation

$$G = \frac{m_1 \, m_2}{d^2}$$ where m_1 and m_2 represent the masses of the particles

and d the distance between them.

For purposes of geography the interaction between two towns might be theoretically expressed in the equation

$$I = \frac{P^1 \, P^2}{d^2}$$ where P^1 and P^2 are the populations of the towns and d

the distance between them. A statement of this degree of precision is clearly open to investigation and modification, but the formula has value in calculating theoretical relationships between settlements. 'Interaction' may, for example, take the form of commuting, journeys for shopping and recreation, or road traffic flows. Some manifestations of the interaction of large towns like Reading and Worcester with surrounding townships and villages can be investigated by pupils—for example the distribution of local newspapers, deliveries from wholesalers or large-store retailers, or daily bus journeys. An understanding of 'interaction' in this sense is valuable

---

[14] See Tidswell and Barker *Quantitative Methods; Geography, a socio-economic approach*, U T P 1971.

if pupils are to appreciate some of the larger issues involved in planning such as the city-region concept and priorities in the building of motorways. A variant of this formula can be used to establish the 'point of break' between two service centres. Points of break are used to define the spheres of influence of towns—an important socio-economic factor widely used in planning.[15]

In the compass of a single chapter it is not possible to do more than suggest a few of the ways in which school geography is moving towards a greater use of theory and mathematical techniques designed to open up new methods and areas of enquiry. If the quality of work is to be enhanced the pupils must be involved in the formulation of problems and their solution. The acid test of theoretical geography is that it should illuminate reality. If it fails to do this it will be of little use to the great majority of the boys and girls whose need is not to pursue an academic discipline but to understand their world. But for those pupils who enter higher education a scientifically and mathematically based study of geography provides a satisfying intellectual experience and a necessary foundation for more advanced studies.

---

[15] See Berry *Geography of Market Centers and Retail Distribution* Prentice Hall 1967.

9

Geography and the Teacher

'The object of any act of learning, over and above the pleasure it may give, is that it should serve us in the future. Learning should not only take us somewhere: it should allow us later to go further more easily'.[1]

At the beginning of Chapter 2 some simple aims of geography teaching in schools were stated. Succeeding pages have dealt with the development of the subject from the primary school to later stages of the secondary school, incorporating by implication suggestions for syllabus-making and ways of teaching.

It may now be possible to analyse the objectives and structure which have been set forth in preceding chapters. These objectives involve skills, attitudes, vocabulary, a variety of elements with which the geographer is concerned, simple relationships, classifications, systems, general concepts and theories. For the purpose of this analysis some of the terms used are self-explanatory, for example, skills, vocabulary and attitudes. Other terms may merit explanation since they are here used in a special, and to some extent arbitrary, sense as they apply to school geography.

The term 'elements' includes the array of things in themselves, and processes associated with them, with which the geography teacher deals. An exhaustive list is not possible in the compass of a pamphlet but the following lists will illustrate what is implied by the term.

Stream, river, lake, estuary, current waterfall, watershed, catchment area; hill, escarpment, plateau, mountain, valley, fiord, glacier, lava, volcanic eruption, cliff, beach, bay, waves; erosion, transportation, deposition.

Air, rain, snow, ice, frost, cloud, wind, temperature, precipitation, air-mass, lapse-rate.

Latitude, Tropic, degrees, International date-line, rotation of the earth.

---

[1] J. S. Bruner *The Process of Education.*

Rock, sand, gravel, clay; soil, humus, soil horizon, solifluction; forest, grassland, tundra, perma-frost.

Field, meadow, wheat, rice, cattle, dairying, ploughing, irrigation, tractor, market.

Iron-ore, bauxite, coal, steel, smelting, quarrying, cotton, spinning, weaving.

Larch, spruce, pulp, paper-making.

Oil, electricity supply, hydro-electric power.

Shop, house, supermarket, chain-store, bank, factory, railway, road, lorry, ship, dock.

The ease with which elements may be understood varies not only with each child and the nature of the environment in which he lives, but also with the complexity of the elements themselves.

Classifications and systems become useful when the reasons for classifying and systematising gain meaning. Trees may be divided into coniferous and broad-leaved, timber into soft-woods and hard-woods, rocks into permeable and impermeable, farms into arable, stock and mixed, high land into volcanoes, plateaus, residual and young fold mountains. Geography abounds in such classifications.

There is little point in learning classificatory terms unless reasons for making distinctions between one class and another are apparent. With younger children simple differences of function or appearance may provide sufficient justification for a classification. Thus the distinction between villages, market towns and large service centres may be, at first, interpreted in terms of size, the number of shops and the amount of traffic; at a later stage a more complex understanding of systems of settlements may emerge. The elements of weather may lead to classifications of rainfall and temperature regimes; these lead to climatic classifications which in turn develop into climatic systems. Systems may apply to single elements—road systems, farming systems, river systems—or to classes as in the case of climates, relief features, or manufacturing regions. It is systems which give pattern to the distribution of phenomena and activities on the earth's surface.

Relationships are basic to geography teaching. When children begin to ask why one thing differs from another they are at the beginning of the process of establishing relationships. The growing of rice or cacao or rubber trees may be related to particular kinds of climates in particular places, different kinds of natural vegetation may be related to different climates, a port may be related to the area it serves, motorways to centres of dense population in highly developed areas, high mountains to difficulties of land communications. Relationships of these kinds are best educed from empirical studies of real places.

When pupils begin to appreciate that, given a similar set of elements, a similar set of relationships exist among them, they are entering into the phase of understanding geographical concepts. Similarly an appreciation of the repetition of systems contributes to an understanding of concepts. The word 'concept' is often used in two quite distinct ways. In one context it has a psychological connotation. It may be said that a pupil has a concept of Mount Everest, or India, or London, and this concept or mental image, is conditioned by his interpretation of the information which he possesses. It is, in fact, personal to him. The term 'geographical concept' is used in an epistemological sense; it is concerned with the ordering of knowledge into recurring patterns and relationships. The pupil who has been led to understand that certain kinds of agricultural response are associated with certain conditions of soil, relief, climate, markets and degrees of development has arrived at an important set of agricultural concepts. The study of ports leads to the concept of hinterlands, of patterns of villages, towns and cities, to concepts of settlement, of mines, quarries, factories and transport to the concept of industrial regions, of poor and rich nations to the concept of underdeveloped areas. The recurring patterns of mountains, plains and rivers, and of climatic distribution are all important concepts in physical geography.

The tropics, the Polar regions, the Moslem world are conceptual a set of understood related ideas which can be applied to many frameworks. The value of such concepts is that they provide regions. It may be useful to analyse the use of terms in geography. Sometimes a word which describes an element may be used in a conceptual sense. For example a fiord coast is a complicated element in geography, but a teacher may use the term 'fiord-coast' in a conceptual sense implying a complex act of relationships which may properly be applied to parts of New Zealand, Southern Chile, British Columbia and Norway.

Models and theories have been dealt with at some length in Chapter 8. The study of a particular place with specific characteristics or a sequence of development, may be used as a model with which other similar regions or points in a sequence may be compared. These may be regarded as real models. But theoretical models too have their value in that they require pupils to apply relationships and concepts to a theoretical situation such as the building of a factory, the expansion of an existing town or the creation of a new one, or the construction of a network of communications; they can also be applied in physical geography. Their value lies in the need for creative and analytical thinking in which lessons learned from the real world can be brought to bear on the solution of problems. They call for the careful examination and evaluation of data, of a kind similar to that experienced in real situations, but now applied within familiar frameworks of thinking to novel situations. Thus they relate the empirical-inductive modes of thought to the theoretical-deductive. In school geography they would represent little more than an interesting academic exercise if they stopped at this point; but if they are used as a yard-stick by which reailty is tested they reveal those elements and relationships which contribute to the uniqueness of each place.

The argument for the sequence of development in school geography may be shown diagrammatically.

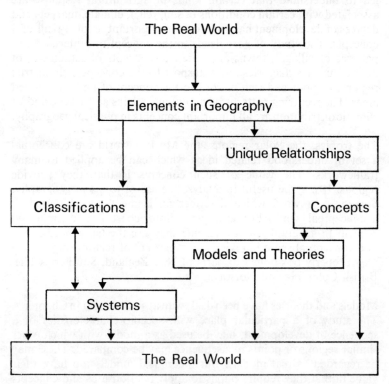

Figure 12.

The starting place is the real world where the basic components, elements and associated vocabulary, may be comprehended. At every stage the real world contributes to the structuring of elements in to orderly groupings and relationships which, in turn, support the growth of general concepts, theories and models. These are used to illuminate the real world. The structure of school geography ends, where it begins, in studies of real places; its justification is that it offers progression of thought and a sense of world perspective, its aims are the solution of problems of the environment.

In constructing a syllabus of work it is the teacher's responsibility to ensure that the range of experience of the pupils is constantly widened, that the systematic ordering of knowledge and an appreciation of relationships are encouraged at the appropriate time, and that the more mature modes of thought represented by concepts, systems, models and theories are nurtured. For some pupils this stage may be reached late in their school life; a few may never reach it. But this is no reason for holding back those who reveal powers of analysis and logical thinking earlier in their school life. Progression in the quality of geographical thinking will only be achieved if the teacher is aware of its nature and actively pursues it.

The generous help of many schools and teachers is gratefully acknowledged. Examples of their work appear anonymously throughout this pamphlet.